Patrick Scheurle

Predictability of the Swiss Stock Market with Respect to Style

GABLER RESEARCH

Patrick Scheurle

Predictability of the Swiss Stock Market with Respect to Style

GABLER

RESEARCH

Bibliographic information published by the Deutsche Nationalbibliothek
The Deutsche Nationalbibliothek lists this publication in the Deutsche Nationalbibliografie; detailed bibliographic data are available in the Internet at http://dnb.d-nb.de.

Dissertation Universität St. Gallen, 2010

1st Edition 2010

Editorial Office: Ute Wrasmann | Sabine Schöller

Gabler is part of the specialist publishing group Springer Science+Business Media.
www.gabler.de

Cover design: KünkelLopka Medienentwicklung, Heidelberg
Printed on acid-free paper
Printed in Germany

ISBN 978-3-8349-2191-8

Preface

A prerequisite for a doctoral thesis is an initial idea that merits examination. My studies at the University of St.Gallen allowed me to develop such an idea. In particular, I am grateful to having met Professor Klaus Spremann who inspired me and who helped me to link my passion for finance to academic challenges. It was and still is a great experience to work with him. Hence, first and foremost, my deepest gratitude goes to Professor Klaus Spremann. I also thank Professor Andreas Grüner for co-supervising this study and adding to it with his thoughtful comments and suggestions.

My time as a research associate at the Swiss Institute of Banking and Finance was enriched by my colleagues. I thank Alexander Bönner, Roman Frick, Lin Gao, Markus Harlacher, Sebastian Lang, Roman Meyer, and Marina Piantoni for a positive and stimulating working environment. Likewise I thank Professor Pascal Gantenbein for valuable conversations on finance and beyond. Moreover, I thank all participants of our internal research seminars for their constructive feedback. I am also thankful to Nadine Balmer, Olga Beregova, Thomas Hug, Nepomuk Feser, Béatrice Peier and Marc Wink for lively discussions on many topics. A special thank goes to Stephan Hostettler who provided me with useful and generous support. On this note I thank Matthias Bachmann, Roger Bundi, Daniel Gasser, and Andreas Waser for their long lasting friendship which helped keeping the mental balance while working on this dissertation.

Finally, I thank my godfather Hans-Jörg Widmer, my grandfather Max Höliner, my father Eugen, my mother Maya, and my brother Thomas for their unlimited encouragement and support. Their contribution to the success of this thesis is invaluable.

Zurich, November 2009 Patrick Scheurle

Overview of Contents

Contents

Executive Summary

There is evidence of fairly strong serial correlation in small caps and a lead-lag relationship between large caps and small caps. A double ranking according to size and price-to-book ratios allows the separation of small caps and large caps into finer market segments such as small value stocks or large growth stocks. Hence, one might wonder whether large value or large growth stocks lead the returns of small caps and of which small caps. Due to the concept of implied cross-autocorrelation this question can be directed from cross-serial correlation to serial correlation. Moreover, the discussion of a risk premium for cyclical risks which are captured by small caps and value stocks leads to a new point of view. Based on monthly data for the Swiss Stock Market, I investigate to what extent the returns of combined style portfolios are serially correlated and if this serial correlation can be exploited in profitable investment strategies.

My empirical research shows significant positive first-order serial correlation in the returns of large value stocks, large neutral stocks, small neutral stocks, and small growth stocks. Serial correlation seems to have become less significant in the more recent past. Moreover, serial correlation changes over time. The positive autocorrelation in the returns of large value stocks and the average small cap seem to be the most consistent. In the course of testing for profitable investment strategies, two pairs of style rotation strategies are introduced. The most pronounced outperformance in terms of a multifactor Alpha amounts to 9.4% on an annualised basis.

The most challenging question might be where the predictability, i.e., the significant serial correlation comes from. Market frictions, a partial adjustment to new information, and time-varying risk premia are frequently discussed explanations. I offer an explanation which is based on time-varying risk premia and accounts for the possibility of cyclical risks not captured by the CAPM.

Executive Summary (German)

Zahlreiche empirische Arbeiten zeigen serielle Korrelation in den Renditen von Small Caps sowie eine Lead-Lag-Beziehung zwischen Large Caps und Small Caps. Ein doppeltes Ranking nach Unternehmensgrösse und Book-to-Market-Ratio erlaubt eine feinere Einteilung dieser Marktsegmente. So ergeben sich Subsegmente wie beispielsweise kleine Value Stocks oder grosse Wachstumstitel. Somit wird auch die Untersuchung von Lead-Lag-Beziehungen für feinere Marktsegmente ermöglicht. Das Konzept der impliziten Kreuz-Autokorrelation erlaubt es, die Untersuchung von Lead-Lag-Beziehungen auf die Analyse von serieller Korrelation zu fokussieren. Darüber hinaus führt die Diskussion um zyklische Risiken, welche scheinbar insbesondere für Small Caps und Value Stocks relevant sind, zu einer neuen Sichtweise.

Basierend auf monatlichen Daten für den schweizerischen Aktienmarkt wird untersucht, inwieweit serielle Korrelation in kombinierten Style-Portfolios vorzufinden ist und ob diese serielle Korrelation mittels Anlagestrategien ausgenutzt werden kann. Die Ergebnisse meiner Untersuchung zeigen signifikante Autokorrelation in den Renditen von grossen Value Stocks, grossen neutralen Titeln, kleinen neutralen Titeln und kleinen Wachstumstiteln. Serielle Korrelation scheint in der jüngeren Vergangenheit tendenziell abgenommen zu haben. Grundsätzlich scheint serielle Korrelation jedoch zeitvariabel zu sein. Als besonders konstant zeigt sich die positive serielle Korrelation in den Renditen von grossen Value Stocks und von Small Caps. Gemessen an einem Multifaktor-Alpha weisen die untersuchten Anlagestrategien teilweise eine signifikante Outperformance aus.

Häufig genannte Ursachen für serielle Korrelation sind Marktfriktionen, eine partielle Anpassung an neue Informationen sowie zeitvariable Risikoprämien. Ich offeriere eine Erklärung, welche auf zeitvariablen Risikoprämien beruht und dabei die Möglichkeit von zyklischen Risiken, welche im CAPM nicht berücksichtigt werden, miteinbezieht.

List of Figures

List of Tables

Notations and Abbreviations

AMEX	American Stock Exchange
BH	Big High
BM	Big Medium
BL	Big Low
C	Constant
CAPM	Capital Asset Pricing Model
EMH	Efficient Markets Hypothesis
FF	Fama French
GDP	Gross Domestic Product
HML	High Minus Low
i.e.	Id est (that is)
IID	Independently and Identically Distributed
IOS	Investment Opportunity Set
ISIN	International Securities Identification Number
MKT	A market index
NYSE	New York Stock Exchange
p.	Page
pp.	Pages
SH	Small High
SM	Small Medium
SMB	Small Minus Big
SL	Small Low
SPI	Swiss Performance Index
SWX	Swiss Exchange
UMD	Up Minus Down
US	United States (of America)
VMG	Value Minus Growth
WML	Winners Minus Losers

a_k	Intercept in a regression analysis
β_P	Beta
ε	Error term
σ_P	Standard deviation of portfolio returns
ϕ_i	Exposure

$Alpha_P$	Jensen's Alpha
b_k	Exposure to MKT_t
BH_t	Return of the portfolio BH at t
BM_t	Return of the portfolio BM at t
BL_t	Return of the portfolio BL at t
c_k	Exposure to SMB_t
d_k	Exposure to HML_t
HML_t	Return of the portfolio HML at t
IR	Information Ratio
MKT_t	Return of the portfolio MKT at t
$P_{k,t}$	Risk premium of k at t
R^2	R-squared measure
R_0	Risk free rate
R_G	Return of a benchmark portfolio G
R_P	Return of a portfolio P
SH_t	Return of the portfolio SH at t
SM_t	Return of the portfolio SM at t
SMB_t	Return of the portfolio SMB at t
SL_t	Return of the portfolio SL at t
$SR(P)$	Sharpe Ratio of a portfolio P

t	A point in time or a time period
TE	Tracking error
$TR(P)$	Treynor Ratio of a portfolio P
x_{t-1}	Lagged variable
y_t	Dependent variable
y_{t-1}	Lagged dependent variable

1. Introduction

1.1. Motivation

The world of finance has changed a lot during the past decades. Empirical research and sophisticated econometric tests have revealed new insights into how financial markets work. Modern Portfolio Theory has been enriched with a multi factor perspective leading to more complexity and accuracy at the same time. Moreover, market efficiency and stock return predictability do not seem to be purely contrasting ideas anymore. However, the ultimate answer to the question whether stock returns are predictable or not and how possible return predictability is linked to market efficiency and the real economy has not been found so far. With this work I seek to contribute to this field of research.

Lo and MacKinlay (1989; 1990a; 1990b) and others report fairly strong serial correlation in small caps and a lead-lag relationship between large caps and small caps. Other research shows the forecasting power of the dividend-price ratio and similar valuation measures such as the book-to-market ratio. In many cases the research on forecasting is restricted to aggregate market returns or to a broad group of stocks such as small caps or large caps. To my knowledge, there are only a few articles on the predictability of the returns of other style portfolios like value and growth. The factor mimicking portfolios of Fama and French (1993) may help in two ways to further investigate the serial correlation in the returns of certain styles such as small caps or value stocks. First, the construction approach of the Fama-French-Portfolios allows a more detailed investigation of style portfolios. While classical style concepts consider small caps, large caps, value stocks, and growth stocks, the Fama-French Approach allows a sophisticated refinement of these styles. Due to a double ranking according to size and book-to-market values, there appear six intersectional portfolios ranging from small value stocks to large growth stocks, i.e., combined style portfolios are created. This opens a new level of analysis. Second, these combined style portfolios are the cornerstones of the risk factors SMB and HML. Taking risks associated with SMB and

HML is rewarded by a risk premium. However, the discussion of the risk sources behind SMB and HML is not yet closed. A growing body of research, for instance, Cochrane (1999a; 2005a, pp. 442-444), points out the possibility of macroeconomic risks which are captured by the two risk factors. In other words, particular styles which appear in a risk factor that might capture risks associated with the real economy are reported to have highly serially correlated returns. This calls for further investigations. More recent research extends Cochrane's interpretation. Spremann and Scheurle (2009), for instance, link the risk factors SMB and HML to different stages of the business cycle. In addition to these new perspectives, combined style portfolios like small value or large growth seem to have been neglected in research as well as in practice. For instance, Lewellen (2002) or Fama and French (2007a; 2007b) show how little we know about these portfolios and how much possible research is still left. The above-mentioned findings on (cross-)serial correlation and the ongoing interest in the Fama-French Factors and their associated risks provide a strong incentive for further research.

I focus on the Swiss stock market, which may be regarded as a developed financial market. However, the Swiss stock market has some peculiarities. For instance, a small number of stocks represent a major part of the entire market capitalisation. In contrast, many companies listed in Switzerland show a very low market capitalisation with poor trading activity in their stocks. These characteristics of the Swiss stock market provide a special motivation and might be of additional interest in a discussion of predictability in stock returns.

1.2. Research Idea

The starting point of my research is the observation by Lo and MacKinlay (1990a) of a lead-lag relationship between large caps and small caps, with returns of large caps leading the returns of small caps. However, with the above-mentioned research of Fama and French in mind, one might wonder whether large value or large growth stocks lead the returns of small caps and of which small caps. Moreover, Boudoukh, Richardson, and Whitelaw (1994) introduce the concept of implied cross-serial correlation which enables a break-down of lead-lag relationships into autocorrelation and contemporaneous correlation between stock returns. Hence, lead-lag relationships would be another way to describe correlation and autocorrelation coefficients. In other words, high cross-serial correlations might be due to high correlations, high serial correlation, or both. Contemporaneous correlation is usually high among stock returns. Thus, an investigation of this kind of correlation seems unappealing and an analysis of serial correlation might be more favourable. However, serial correlation is in contrast with the random walk model, which is widely assumed to hold for stock returns. Loosely speaking, the random walk model describes how returns are generated. An important characteristic of the random walk model is the unpredictability of returns. Stock prices react to new information, and as new information appears randomly, stock prices must react randomly, too.

$$(1) \qquad y = f(x)$$

In equation (1) the variable x follows a random walk. Hence, y is not predictable. However, there are competing models which allow for predictability. Due to the concept of implied cross-serial correlation, the question of which large caps lead which small caps may be reduced to the question of which portfolios have the highest correlation and the highest autocorrelation. As high correlation among stock returns is the rule rather than the exception, I set the focus on serial correlation and thus on the random walk model.

I follow the research covering the Fama-French Factors and the predictable returns field and test whether the returns of the Fama-French Factors or of components of those factors are predictable to some extent. More precisely, in a first step I test for serial correlation in the returns of the Fama-French Portfolios. In other words, I test for autocorrelation in the returns of various combined style portfolios such as small value or large growth. These combined style portfolios have been shown to be of great interest with respect to the relationship between financial markets and the real economy. Consequently, I intend to obtain new insights into the connection of market efficiency, return predictability, and macroeconomics. In particular, I aim to answer two research questions.

Research question 1:

> *Are the returns of the Fama-French factor-mimicking Portfolios or of components of these portfolios applicable in stock return forecasting?*

With research question 1 I follow two ideas. The first involves using past returns of the Fama-French Portfolios as predictor variables. The second idea involves breaking down the forecasting level from a market perspective to a style or a market segment perspective. As mentioned above, a large amount of research focuses on the predictability of aggregate stock market returns. I focus on the predictability of certain market segments such as small caps or value stocks and even finer market segments such as small value stocks. Breaking down the level of analysis might be particularly relevant for the interpretation of the results with respect to the previously mentioned risk factors and a possible relationship between stock return predictability and the real economy.

However, the concept of implied cross-serial correlation might neglect certain aspects. For example, the estimated empirical values of cross-autocorrelations usually deviate from their implied counterparts. Hence, estimated cross-serial correlation could be able to capture some information which may be meaningful in stock return predictability. This might be interesting with respect to investment strategies. This and the interest in the economic magnitude of potential predictability lead me to the second research question.

Research question 2:

Is it possible to create profitable investment strategies based on estimated (cross-)serial correlations among the Fama-French Portfolios?

The required analyses in order to answer the second research question might be interesting with respect to two points. First, the evaluation of investment strategies points to the economic significance of possible predictability as it is not restricted to statistical measures. Second, there might be additional information on the meaning of the difference between estimated and implied cross-serial correlation.

In order to being able to contribute to the above-mentioned areas of research, the stated research questions will be reformulated as hypotheses at the beginning of the empirical parts. The reformulation enables a rejection or acceptance of the research hypotheses.

1.3. Outline

Chapter 2 provides a literature review which covers research on factor-mimicking portfolios and serial correlation as well as related research on return predictability. A theoretical framework is presented in Chapter 3. Chapter 4 outlines the research methodology and provides descriptive statistics of the sample data. Chapter 5 presents empirical results on serial correlation in the returns of the Fama-French Portfolios. In chapter 6 I develop the forecasting models which are applied in the investment strategies of Chapter 7. Chapter 8 concludes the work.

2. Literature Review

2.1. Structure of Literature Review

The present chapter will provide an overview of the relevant literature on factor-mimicking portfolios and return predictability. However, the literature, especially on the forecastability of returns, is extensive and therefore, the research mentioned can represent no more than a selection. In order to provide a more comprehensive picture of return predictability I do not restrict the literature review to serial correlation.

The following section covers some literature on factor-mimicking portfolios and their relationship to macroeconomic risks. This point is frequently taken up in the course of this book. The subsequent section provides an overview of the literature about return predictability. Since the empirical research presented in later chapters is based on (cross-)serial correlation I especially focus on the literature from this specific field. Nevertheless, in order to give a more thorough picture of this vivid research area, I also provide an overview of other forecasting ideas. Moreover, possible predictability on the basis of past returns might be related to other forecasting variables. For instance, ratios such as the price-to-book ratio can have predictive power because of changes in price, book values, or both. Hence, in the first of the three cases the possible forecasting power of such ratios could be reduced to predictive power of price changes and thus returns. In addition, certain forecasting ideas laid the foundation for "economic" tests of return predictability (Campbell, Lo, and MacKinlay (1997, p. 42)). Therefore, serial and cross-serial correlation may not be an island within the predictable returns field. However, a reader interested mainly in (cross-) autocorrelation might concentrate on section 2.3.5. and skip the other parts of the literature review.

As mentioned above, the literature on return predictability is extensive. I therefore structure the research on return predictability according to its predictor variables. However, the classification is not always able to provide clear-cut categories for the research as some papers cover predictor variables across different classes. Therefore, section 2.3.1. also contains research based on predictors of multiple classes.

Another important aspect in the field of return predictability is the Efficient Market Hypothesis. Researchers in this field have also been very active, producing dozens of articles. A brief literature review on market efficiency is provided in the next chapter along the outline of the foundations of the Efficient Market Hypothesis.

2.2. Factor-Mimicking Portfolios and Macroeconomics

Chen, Roll, and Ross (1986) show the importance of macroeconomic variables in explaining the risk premium of stock returns. In their research, Chen, Roll, and Ross (1986) consider factors such as the growth rate of industrial production, unexpected changes in credit spreads or unexpected changes in term spreads.[1] However, macroeconomic variables do have some drawbacks such as, for instance, their low publication frequency. This is especially striking if the low frequency coincides with short time series. Fama and French (1993) present a new form of risk factors. Instead of applying macroeconomic variables directly, they use portfolio-based factors which, according to today's state of research, might capture the effects of macroeconomic fluctuations. However, Cochrane (2005b, pp. 6-7) identifies a division of labour between portfolio models and macroeconomic models. Portfolio models are able to detect whether or not particular asset classes have a common movement with the risk factors. Macroeconomic models help to understand why the portfolio-based risk factors are priced.

The portfolio-based approach of Fama and French (1993) and its link to the real economy received much attention and was subsequently enriched and extended. In the following, I present selected research on factor-mimicking portfolios and their relationship to macroeconomics.

[1] Note that they did not replace the market index as a risk factor but extended the model with additional variables.

Fama and French (1993) use the returns of two long-short portfolios as additional risk factors besides a proxy for the market portfolio. Their multifactor model is given below.

(2) $$P_{k,t} = a_k + b_k \cdot MKT_t + c_k \cdot SMB_t + d_k \cdot HML_t + \varepsilon$$

There are $k = 1, 2, ..., n$ assets. $P_{k,t}$ is the excess return, i.e., the risk premium of asset k at t. MKT_t, SMB_t, and HML_t are returns at t. SMB is an abbreviation for Small Minus Big. It is a portfolio which is long in small caps and short in large caps. The other portfolio is called HML, which stands for High Minus Low.[2] This second portfolio is long in value stocks and short in growth stocks. High and low refer to the book-to-market ratio.[3] As in Chen, Roll, and Ross (1986), the one-factor model is extended by additional factors. There still is a proxy for the market portfolio. Fama and French (1993) detect significant explanatory power and positive risk premia of the two new factors for US returns. The research was also conducted for international equity markets. For instance, Fama and French (1998) test HML for markets around the world. However, given the observation of the small cap effect by Banz (1981) and Reinganum (1981) and the detection of relatively high returns of value stocks compared to growth stocks by Stattman (1980), the positive expected returns of the long-short portfolios do not seem surprising. Nonetheless, the rationale for the risk premia on the long-short portfolios described might not be obvious.

Cochrane (1999a) provides a reasonable explanation for these risk premia. The average investor is already exposed to macroeconomic risk. Heaton and Lucas (2000) point out the large fraction of stockholders who run small, privately held businesses. This group of shareholders faces substantial exposure to changes in the macroeconomic environment. Hence, such investors are not willing to hold assets which decline at the same time when their business is at risk and all other assets loose value. Based on Fama and French (1996), it is argued that small caps and value stocks seem to have an especially high exposure to business activity and therefore carry a risk

[2] In Fama and French (2006) HML is called VMG which stands for Value Minus Growth.
[3] Value stocks have high book-to-market ratios and growth stocks have low book-to-market ratios.

premium. However, there are other explanations as well. Lakonishok, Shleifer, and Vishny (1994) attribute the high returns of value stocks and the low returns of growth stocks to the suboptimal behaviour of the typical investor. A more concrete reason for the high returns of value stocks is given by La Porta, Lakonishok, Shleifer, and Vishny (1997). Their research suggests an important role of earnings announcement return differences between value and growth stocks. Again, these differences are attributed to behavioural aspects such as expectational errors and not to possible risks overlooked by the CAPM.

Following the Fama and French's (1993) idea researchers tested various other factor-mimicking portfolios. Carhart (1997) uses the findings of Jegadeesh and Titman (1993) to create a momentum factor and extends the Fama-French Model to a four-factor model.

(3) $$r_{it} = a_{iT} + b_{iT} \cdot RMRF_t + s_{iT} \cdot SMB_t + h_{iT} \cdot HML_t + p_{iT} \cdot PR1YR_t + e_{it}$$

The excess return r_{it} of a portfolio i in the period t is regressed on the four factors $RMRF_t$, SMB_t, HML_t, and $PR1YR_t$. The first three factors represent the Fama-French Factors. $PR1YR_t$ is the return of a zero-investment portfolio which is long in stocks with a strong performance during the previous year and short in stocks with a poor performance in the previous year. There are similar momentum factors such as UMD or WML. UMD stands for Up Minus Down. UMD is a portfolio which is long in stocks with a strong performance in the previous six to nine weeks and short in stocks with a weak performance in the previous six to nine weeks. Rouwenhorst (1998) tested a factor WML, Winners Minus Losers, in an international context and supports the momentum effect. Ammann and Steiner (2008) investigate the Carhart Factors for the Swiss stock market. Liew and Vassalou (2000) test the predictive power of MKT, SMB, HML, and WML for GDP growth. They find that SMB and HML add significant predictability to MKT but WML does not. Moreover, the significance does not vanish as other business cycle variables such as the term spread are included in the analysis. The research of Liew and Vassalou (2000) also opens new horizons. SMB and HML are constructed of several market segments. Hence, it may be possible to trace the predictive power of the risk factors to finer market segments.

Unfortunately, it is not yet entirely clear which macroeconomic risks are associated with the above-described risk factors. Nevertheless, the growing body of research suggests a relationship between the above-outlined factor-mimicking portfolios and the real economy. Moreover, the explanation of risks associated with SMB and HML can be better interpreted than risks possibly associated with momentum factors. Fama and French (1996) question whether the momentum effect is real or not. Cochrane (1999a) outlines the possibility of a statistical anomaly which arises from tiny positive serial correlation of returns and may generate momentum profits. Vassalou and Apedjinou (2004) apply a factor called HLCI which explains much of the performance of momentum strategies. HLCI is an abbreviation for High Minus Low Corporate Innovation. HLCI is the return of a portfolio which is long in innovative firms and short in less innovative firms. It seems that corporate innovation is an important aspect of return continuation. However, Cochrane (2005b, pp. 21-23) still considers momentum as an anomaly.

2.3. Literature on Return Predictability

2.3.1. Macroeconomic Variables

The above literature on factor-mimicking portfolios might indicate the meaning of macroeconomic variables in order to explain (stock) returns. Several researchers have investigated the possible predictability of returns by using variables from the real economy. Bodie (1976) found a negative relation between real returns and expected inflation, i.e., expected inflation could be used to forecast stock returns. Nelson (1976) and Fama and Schwert (1977) support this conclusion. Jaffe and Mandelker (1976) find possible forecasting power from inflation, at least in some time intervals. Fama (1981) concludes that inflation serves as a proxy for real activity.

Fama and French (1989) find predictive power in dividend yields, default spreads, and time spreads for stock and bond returns. They relate their findings to business conditions. In times of poor economic performance expected returns must be high in order to motivate people to allocate income to investments instead of consumption. The predictive power of the dividend yield, the credit spread, and the term spread is also documented by Fama (1990). Balvers, Cosimano, and McDonald (1990) highlight the possibility of predictable returns in an efficient market. As aggregate output is serially correlated and thus predictable, asset returns have to be predictable as well. The link between predictable output and predictable returns is people's desire to smooth consumption over time. In order to smooth consumption people adjust their required rate of return. For instance, if people anticipate lower output, and hence lower consumption opportunities in the next period they will try to transfer wealth to that period. Hence, people accept a lower rate of return as a consequence of their reluctance to volatile consumption streams. A similar conclusion is presented by Chen (1991). State variables such as the dividend yield forecasts economic activity and economic activity forecasts the market premium.

2.3.2. Valuation Ratios

Research on the predictive power of dividend yields may have started with Rozeff (1984) who investigated the forecasting power of dividend yields and concluded that returns did not follow a random walk. Supportive arguments on this conclusion are given by Shiller (1984). Fama and French (1988b) conduct in-sample and out-of-sample tests for the predictive power of the dividend-price ratio. They test forecasts for return horizons ranging from one month to five years and find increasing predictability for longer horizons. A possible explanation for this finding is also introduced: The discount-rate effect. Shocks to expected returns cause opposite shocks to current prices, thus affecting the variance of the regression residuals. Campbell and Shiller (1988) apply long moving averages of earnings and the relationship of these to prices. They find this kind of earnings-price ratio to be a powerful forecasting variable for stock returns, especially for multi-year returns. Fama (1990) confirms the predictive power of the dividend yield. Pontiff and Schall (1998) investigate return predictability of aggregate book-to-market ratios in US data. Their evidence shows the predictive power of the book-to-market ratio. However, forecasting power seems to be considerably stronger in the period before 1960. Moreover, aggregate ratios of the S&P index seem to be stronger than aggregate ratios of the Dow Jones Industrial Index. In the post-1960 period only the book-to-market ratio of the S&P index retains significant predictive power. Lamont (1998) finds predictive power in dividends as well as in earnings. Lamont (1998) links the explanatory power of earnings to business conditions. High earnings signal favourable business conditions, which induce investors to require lower expected returns. In contrast, the reason for the explanatory power of dividends seems less clear. However, for forecasting long-horizon returns, dividends and earnings might be less important than (scaled) stock prices. Campbell and Shiller (1998) investigate the predictability of long-run returns. In particular, they analyse whether long-run predictability is due to changes in the numerator or denominator of certain valuation ratios such as the dividend-price ratio. This shows the close relationship between research on the predictive power of valuation ratios and research on serial correlation in returns. With respect to the dividend-price ratio, Campbell and Shiller (1998) document that price movements are responsible for the mean reverting characteristic of this ratio. However, the evidence from real data does not coincide with results from simulations which show a stronger effect of dividend growth rates. Cochrane (1999b) summarizes research which is based on the dividend price ratio. In particular, he shows three implications of predictable returns: Horizon effects, market timing, and hedging demands. With respect to market timing, he emphasises the work of Brandt (1999), Campbell and Vicera (1999), Brennan, Schwartz, and Lagnado (1997). Asness, Friedman, Krail, and Liew (2000) develop a model which is intended to predict the returns of value and growth stocks. They identify differentials in earnings-to-price ratios, book-to-price ratios, and sales-to-price ratios as important input variables. Goyal and Welch (2003) also investigate the predictive power of dividend ratios. They apply annual US data from 1926 to 2002 and find no predictive power in dividend ratios for horizons shorter than five years. In contrast, Lewellen (2004) finds strong predictive power for dividend yields in using

US data from 1946 to 2000 if one corrects the small-sample bias. Further, Cochrane (2006) extends the discussion of statistical issues when testing for predictability. He points out that the absence of dividend growth predictability yields much stronger evidence on return predictability. Goyal and Welch (2006) reexamine the predictive power of various ratios. Their research does not suggest much help for investors from most of the forecasting models.

2.3.3. Accounting Data

The link between predictability in returns and forecasting on the basis of accounting data seems less clear than a forecast by valuation ratios. Nevertheless, predictability from accounting data may be interesting with respect to the source of serial correlation. Hence, a brief outline of the literature on predictability and accounting data is presented.

Ball and Brown (1968) find that stock returns tend to drift for several months after earnings surprises and that the drift is in the same direction as the earnings surprise. Foster, Olsen, and Tevlin (1984) support this finding with restrictions. Only a few models are able to explain the drift effects. Bernard and Thomas (1989) investigate two competing rationales for this drift effect. One reason for post-earnings-announcement drifts might be delayed information processing by market participants. Another explanation argues that the CAPM does not fully reflect risk, and therefore abnormal returns are determined incorrectly. Bernard and Thomas (1989) conclude that the first reason is more appealing. Shivakumar (2006) highlights the superior forecasting power of future returns of cash flow surprises over earnings surprises.

2.3.4. Calendar Anomalies

Calendar anomalies can distract from other sources of predictability. Often, it is important to account for calendar anomalies in order to separate different effects of predictability. The forecasting models developed in Chapter 6 may also be affected by calendar anomalies. In order to give an idea of how these effects can influence forecasting models, I briefly summarize the evidence on calendar anomalies in this section.

The weekend effect, the January effect, and the monthly effect are three frequently cited calendar anomalies. The weekend effect describes unusually low returns on Mondays and sometimes unusually high returns on Fridays. An early investigation of this effect was conducted by Cross (1973). French (1980) finds the weekend effect to be actually tied to weekends and that it does not hold for other holidays on which markets are closed. Gibbons and Hess (1981), Roll (1983), and Keim and Stambaugh (1984) also identify negative Monday returns. Jaffe and Westerfield (1985) investigate the weekend effect for the US, UK, Japan, Canada, and Australia and find the effect in each of these countries. However, the lowest mean returns in Japan and Australia seem to occur on Tuesday. The January effect states higher mean returns in January than in other months of the year, an effect that was observed and documented by a number of researchers such as Rozeff and Kinney (1976) or Tinic and West (1984). Jegadeesh (1991) reports a January effect for mean reversion in US and UK data. Keim (1983) investigates the January effect with respect to firm size. He finds small caps to have large abnormal returns in January. Moreover, a significant part of the size effect reported by Banz (1981) and Reinganum (1981) seems to be due to the first trading days in January. Reinganum (1983) partially ascribes this anomaly to the tax-loss selling effect. However, this effect is not able to fully explain the high January returns. Further, Keim (1989) identifies closing prices as a partial explanation of calendar anomalies. For instance, closing prices in December are often recorded at bid prices and closing prices in January are often recorded at ask prices. This leads to positive returns even if no changes in bid and ask prices occur. With respect to the monthly effect, Ariel (1987) shows for value-weighted and equally weighted index returns for US data between 1963 and 1981 that most of a month's return occurs in the first half of the month and that the second half of the month contributes almost nothing.

2.3.5. Serial Correlation and Momentum

Early evidence of serial correlation in returns of single stocks was found by Fama (1965). Fisher (1966) finds positive autocorrelation in monthly returns of diversified portfolios. Lo and MacKinlay (1988), Conrad and Kaul (1988), McInish and Wood (1991) as well as Mech (1993) find small cap portfolios to show stronger positive autocorrelation than portfolios consisting of large caps. Jegadeesh (1990) documents significant negative first-order serial correlation among monthly individual stock returns. Lo and MacKinlay (1990a; 1990b) report strong cross-autocorrelation among size-sorted portfolios. Moreover, the asymmetrical correlations suggest lead-lag relationships between certain market segments. Lewellen (2002) investigates autocorrelations and cross-autocorrelations of returns of size and book-to-market sorted portfolios. Additionally, he analyses intersectional portfolios. One finding is the difficulty of differentiating between underreaction and time-varying expected returns as one runs into the joint-hypothesis problem described by Fama (1970). Another finding is the negative serial and cross-serial correlation of size and book-to-market sorted portfolios when correlations of monthly returns and past 12-month returns are used. Lewellen (2002) finds the difference between lead-lag effects and autocorrelation to be a source of momentum profits.

Chan (1993) points out the role of market makers and their processing of information as a reason for cross-autocorrelations among size sorted portfolios. Boudoukh, Richardson, and Whitelaw (1994) offer three possible explanations of why higher autocorrelations of small cap portfolios might occur. First, market frictions such as nonsynchronous trading could lead to apparent (cross-)autocorrelation of returns.[4]

[4] Nonsynchronous trading is also referred to as thin trading or non-trading.

Second, market participants might only partially adjust to new information. Hence, autocorrelation would be induced by a slow incorporation of the news into stock prices. Third, time-varying risk premia could be the source of (cross-)autocorrelation. Boudoukh, Richardson, and Whitelaw (1994) find market frictions to be the most likely reason for cross-serial correlation. This is not entirely in line with the results of Lo and MacKinlay (1990b) and Jegadeesh (1990), who find nonsynchronous trading to affect (cross-)autocorrelations only to a limited extent. Brennan, Jegadeesh, and Swaminathan (1993) analyse the effect of analyst coverage and find that stocks with higher coverage lead those with lower coverage. Moreover, they identify a faster reaction of the high coverage stocks to new common information compared to the stocks followed by fewer analysts. Badrinath, Kale, and Noe (1995) analyse the role of institutional shareholders and conclude that stocks with a high interest of (informed) institutional shareholders lead those stocks held by (uninformed) noninstitutional shareholders. Based on daily and weekly returns and controlling for size effects and thin trading, Chordia and Swaminathan (2000) investigate the effect of trading volume on lead-lag relationships. They find high volume stocks leading low volume stocks. Moreover, this seems to be the case even in the size quintile containing the largest stocks. Chordia and Swaminathan (2000) suggest the speed of adjustment to marketwide information as a reason for lead-lag relationships among volume sorted portfolios. It seems that high volume stocks respond faster to such information than low volume stocks.

Tests of serial correlation and cross-autocorrelation for return frequencies of one year and more were also conducted. Fama and French (1988a) report zero autocorrelation for short return horizons but strong negative serial correlation at return horizons of three to five years. Similarly, Poterba and Summers (1988) find negative autocorrelation for returns at horizons ranging from two to eight years. These findings are also supported by Ball and Kothari (1989). Both, Fama and French (1988a) as well as Poterba and Summers (1988) investigate returns of diversified portfolios. However, with longer return horizons comes weaker statistical power. Fama (1991) provides an overview of earlier research on autocorrelation.

De Bondt and Thaler (1985; 1987) find that stocks which had a poor performance in the previous three to five years are likely to do exceptionally well in the following years. Furthermore, they find extreme winners to underperform the market in the following years. Jegadeesh and Titman (1993) support the findings of De Bondt and Thaler and extend their research to shorter time periods. They report, for instance, a 12.01% annual excess return of an investment strategy which buys the winners of the last 6 months and sells the losers of the past 6 months. The findings of Jegadeesh and Titman (1993) suggest momentum at shorter horizons and mean reversion at longer horizons. Lee and Swaminathan (2000) analyse the relationship between trading volume and momentum. According to their research, volume is able to predict the magnitude as well as the persistence of future price momentum. In addition, they find characteristics of value stocks in low volume stocks. Bhojraj and Swaminathan (2006) consider international equity indices. They support the above-mentioned findings for US Data and present momentum effects after the first year of the portfolio formation period and reversal behaviour during the subsequent 2 years. Moskowitz and Grinblatt (1999) investigate momentum returns of industry sorted portfolios. They find industry-based momentum strategies to be highly profitable. Moreover, they identify the long positions as the main source of profitability which might be interesting for investors with short sales restrictions.

De Bondt and Thaler (1985) ascribe the profitability of contrarian strategies to stock market overreaction. In contrast, Chan (1988) attributes the strong performance of contrarian strategies to time varying betas and risk premia. Ball and Kothari (1989) test whether the negative serial correlation in five-years returns is due to mispricing or due to changing expected returns. Their evidence supports the hypothesis of changing relative risks, which affects expected returns. Conrad, Gultekin, and Kaul (1997) investigate the profitability of short-term contrarian strategies. Their evaluations are based on weekly returns of NASDAQ and NYSE/AMEX stocks. Most of the profitability vanishes as bid/ask bounces and transactions costs are taken into account. With respect to the momentum effect, Chan, Jegadeesh, and Lakonishok (1996) argue that a risk-based explanation is difficult and suggest a gradual response of the market to new information as a more reasonable rationale. Kent, Hirshleifer, and

Subrahmanyam (1998) and Hong and Stein (1999) support an explanation based on under- and overreaction to news. According to Conrad and Kaul (1998), a main determinant of the profitability of momentum strategies are cross-sectional differences in expected returns. However, Jegadeesh and Titman (2001; 2002) and Lewellen (2002) do not agree with this finding. The unconditional mean of past winners and past losers might not be significantly different. Chordia and Shivakamur (2002) find time-varying expected returns a reasonable explanation for momentum. Nevertheless, they do not deny the possibility of behavioural aspects. Korajczyk and Sadka (2004) investigate the robustness of momentum strategies to trading costs. Equal weighted strategies are more sensitive to transaction costs than value-weighted strategies, but overall, momentum strategies remain profitable. Hvidkjaer (2006) shows that initial underreaction and delayed reaction of small traders contribute to the momentum effect. Moskowitz and Grinblatt (1999) mention the possibility of hot industries as a source of the profits of industry-based momentum strategies.

3. Return Predictability and the Real Economy

3.1. Efficient Market Hypothesis

The Efficient Market Hypothesis (EMH) is one part of the foundation of my research. Loosely speaking, the EMH tries to explain how much information is reflected in security prices. An efficient market is supposed to reflect more information than an inefficient one. Fama (1970) formulates an efficient market as follows:

> *«A market in which prices always 'fully reflect' available information is called 'efficient'.»*

In such an informationally efficient market with properly anticipated price changes, stock prices fully incorporate the expectations and information of all market participants. Moreover, price changes must be unforecastable in such a setting (Campbell, Lo, and MacKinlay (1997, p. 31)).

Based on the work of Roberts (1959), Fama (1970) suggests dividing market efficiency into the three categories of weak, semi-strong, and strong market efficiency. The weak form of market efficiency assumes prices to reflect all historical information. The semi-strong form of market efficiency states that all historical and publicly available information is reflected in securities prices. The strong form of market efficiency presumes securities prices to reflect all historical, publicly available, and private information. A detailed treatment of this classification and market efficiency can be found in Spremann (2006, pp. 149-162; 2007, pp. 441-444). The discussion on market efficiency attracted much attention. In his first overview article on efficient capital markets, Fama (1970) states that the research in this area is bountiful, and Fama (1990), in his second overview article on efficient capital markets, recognises that a full literature review is hardly possible because of the extensive work in this field.

The history of the Efficient Market Hypothesis goes back to the year 1900, when the first empirical results on the movements of stock prices were published. Fama (1970) traces the evolution of the Efficient Market Hypothesis and points out that empirical observations led to the development of the EMH. According to Fama (1970), Samuelson (1965) and Mandelbrot (1966) were the first two researchers who were able to link the empirical observations to an economic theory.

3.2. Random Walk

The random walk model is one of the empirical impetuses of the Efficient Market Hypothesis and is often used as a synonym for an efficient stock market. Malkiel (1999) defines a random walk in a stock market as follows:

> *«When the term is applied to the stock market, it means that short-run changes in stock prices cannot be predicted. »*

Expressed differently, the random walk describes how prices react to new information: New information occurs randomly and therefore affects prices in a random manner. If prices are random then returns are random as well, i.e., a return of a stock at t is independent of its return at $t-1$. Another assumption underlying the (classic) random walk model is stationarity. Stationarity means that the distribution of the log-returns does not change over time. The random walk can be illustrated as the process of log-wealth evolution. In discrete time this can be stated as follows:

$$\begin{aligned} &X_0 = Start \\ &X_1 = X_0 + r_1 \\ &X_2 = X_1 + r_2 \\ &\ldots \\ &X_t = X_{t-1} + r_t \end{aligned} \tag{4}$$

At time 0 the future development of log-wealth $X_0, X_1, X_2, ..., X_T$ is uncertain. However, the wealth X_0 at time 0 is known and serves as starting point. For each time period one increment $r_1, r_2, ..., r_T$ is added. Each increment represents an independent drawing out of the same probability distribution. In finance the increments can be considered as log-returns. Hence, a random walk is a discrete time stochastic process (Spremann (2006, pp. 453-454)).

The roots of the idea of stock returns following a random walk go back to the year 1900, when the French mathematician Louis Bachelier, investigating returns of stocks listed on the securities exchange in Paris, recognised the random movements in stock prices. Kendall (1953) was the first to call these movements a random walk. Fama (1970) and Spremann (2007, pp. 200-213) provide a detailed history of the random walk and its link to the Efficient Market Hypothesis.

However, early definitions of the random walk might be too restrictive to capture real world phenomena. Campbell, Lo, and MacKinlay (1997, pp. 27-33) outline three possible versions of the random walk model. Following the work of Campbell, Lo, and MacKinlay (1997), I briefly outline the three versions of the Random Walk Hypothesis.

The first version of the Random Walk Hypothesis (RW1) requires independently and identically distributed (IID) increments. In this version the dynamics of the stochastic process $\{P_t\}$ are given by the equation below.

$$(5) \qquad P_t = \mu + P_{t-1} + \varepsilon_t, \qquad \varepsilon_t \sim \text{IID}(0, \sigma^2)$$

In equation (5) μ represents the drift and $\text{IID}(0, \sigma^2)$ states that ε_t is independently and identically distributed with mean 0 and variance σ^2. A common distributional assumption for the increments ε_t in finance is normality. However, if the conditional distribution of P_t is normal, there is a positive probability for negative P_t. Hence, a normal distribution would allow negative stock prices. In order to circumvent this issue, one can use the logarithm of prices $p_t = \log P_t$. In this case continuously compounded returns are IID normal variates with mean μ and variance σ^2.

$$(6) \qquad p_t = \mu + p_{t-1} + \varepsilon_t, \qquad \varepsilon_t \sim \text{IID } N(0,\sigma^2)$$

The second version of the Random Walk Hypothesis (RW2) is less restrictive and allows for processes where increments may be independent but not identically distributed. Campbell, Lo, and MacKinlay (1997, pp. 32-33) argue that it is implausible to assume a constant probability law of stock prices during a long period of time as there will have been shifts in technology, the economy, and other environmental areas in which stock prices are determined. RW2 is clearly weaker than RW1 as it allows for time-varying volatility, which is also well documented in the literature.[5]

Random Walk Hypothesis three (RW3) is the most general as it allows for dependent but uncorrelated increments. One example is a process where $Cov(\varepsilon_t, \varepsilon_{t-1}) = 0$ for all $k \neq 0$, but $Cov(\varepsilon_t^2, \varepsilon_{t-1}^2) \neq 0$ for some $k \neq 0$. Campbell, Lo, and MacKinlay (1997, p. 33) refer to the RW3 model as the most tested one in the recent empirical literature.

The above discussion points out an interesting aspect. In order to test the random walk model, one has to determine which model is to be tested. Moreover, each of the three versions of the Random Walk Hypothesis requires a test procedure which is geared to the respective peculiarities. Thus, selected tests for the respective random walk models are outlined in Chapter 5 along the empirical investigations on the Random Walk Hypothesis.

[5] See, for example, Mandelbrot (1963), Fama (1965), or Poterba and Summers (1986).

3.3. Predictability and Cyclical Risks

3.3.1. Does the Efficient Market Hypothesis Hold?

This is a question researchers have sought to answer since the formulation of the hypothesis. Testing the EMH is difficult and the ultimate answer has not yet been found. First of all, one has to determine which form of market efficiency will be tested. Spremann (2007, pp. 444-451) provides an overview of the different forms of market efficiency and possible tests, which I briefly summarize in the next passage.

Researchers testing the weak form of market efficiency often test for serial correlation or apply a filter rule based on buy and sell signals to beat the market. In order to test the semi-strong form of market efficiency, one can conduct event studies or again apply filter rules. Often, these rules are based on valuation ratios. Event studies can also be applied to test for the strong form of market efficiency. For instance, one can test for abnormal returns prior to earnings announcements.

As mentioned above, testing the EMH is difficult and associated with some challenges. As pointed out by Jensen (1978), one challenge is the definition of publicly available information. However, this might be a task which can be tackled with a clear description in the research outline. Another, and a much more difficult challenge, is the fact that tests of market efficiency are tests of a joint hypothesis. By testing the EMH with a filter rule, one assumes a certain underlying market model, which leads to a joint hypothesis. A rejection of the joint hypothesis can have two reasons. Either the market is inefficient or the market model does not fully reflect reality. In other words, declining the joint hypothesis does not necessarily mean inefficient markets (Spremann (2007, p. 450)).

The problem of the joint hypothesis has not allowed declining the EMH so far. Fama (1970) concludes that the weak and semi-strong forms are likely to hold. In reference to the strong form of market efficiency, Jensen (1978) states:

«Although there is evidence inconsistent with the Strong Form of the Efficient Market Hypothesis, if there is anything surprising about it, it is the fact that such inconsistent evidence is so scarce.»

Moreover, Jensen (1978) refines the market efficiency definitions with respect to transaction costs. According to this more modern interpretation of market efficiency, there might be situations which appear as market inefficiencies, but as one accounts for transactions costs, the prospective profits disappear. Moreover, as Grossman and Stiglitz (1980) argue, even in theory there may be abnormal returns. The gathering and processing of information is costly but important in order to keep markets efficient. Hence, apparent abnormal returns may be a compensation for the information gathering and processing.

Campbell, Lo, and MacKinlay (1997, p. 24) suggest relative efficiency as a more useful concept than that of perfect efficiency. Relative efficiency measures the efficiency of one market against another, with perfect efficiency as a benchmark which is considered ideal but economically unrealisable. For instance, one market may be closer to the ideal than another market. A similar view is also applicable to return predictability. More recent research no longer tries to interpret possible predictability as evidence against the EMH. Predictable returns might be real and rational (Fama (1990)). Thus, a brief discussion in this direction is provided in the following two sections.

3.3.2. Time-Varying Risk Premia

For returns to be predictable they have to fluctuate over time in a predictable manner or be constant. Indeed, there is little doubt about the fact that expected returns vary over time. Moreover, there is a growing body of research which documents some predictability in expected returns.[6] However, the reason why expected returns may be time-varying is not yet clear.

Schnedler (2003, pp. 317-320) distinguishes between two situations of return predictability. The first situation is one of inefficient markets. Available information is not processed correctly; therefore, inaccurate valuations may occur and prices may be too low or too high. Hence, investors who identify the price deviations can exploit them. Another interpretation is that the price of risk or the risk aversion is not constant over time. In such a setting, even if the condition of efficient markets holds, expected returns may vary in a predictable manner over time. Ferson and Harvey (1991), for example, conclude that predictability may be ascribed to time-varying, rationally expected returns. Along with the identification of additional risk premia, the perspective of predictability in efficient markets has attracted much academic interest. Thus, the situation of predictable returns in efficient markets deserves some extra attention.

The above-presented view may be somewhat sketchy, and the perspective of time-varying risk premia might be of particular interest if we account for more recent research which assumes more than one source of risk, i.e., more than one risk premium. As outlined in the literature review, a frequently discussed source of risk is the exposure to a changing macroeconomic situation. This discussion was initiated by the results of empirical tests of the CAPM. The CAPM by Sharpe (1964) and Lintner (1965) is supposed to capture the risk of a certain security by quantifying its exposure to a single source of risk, namely, the fluctuations of the market portfolio. Early tests of the CAPM, for instance the one by Black, Jensen, and Scholes (1972) or the one by Fama and MacBeth (1973), could not alter this view. However, after the test by Fama and French (1992) the power of the CAPM with respect to the ability to describe the real-world behaviour of investors was put into perspective. The results led in two research directions. The first, behavioural finance, tries to explain the results by the bounded rationality of investors. The other research direction adheres to the foundations of Modern Portfolio Theory but recognizes potential extensions. Investors

[6] Cochrane (2005b, pp. 11-15) provides a survey of literature on time variation of expected returns.

are rational, but a single source of risk does not describe reality appropriately; hence, additional risk factors have to be included. These additional risk factors may help with the interpretation of predictable returns in efficient markets.

As mentioned above, Fama and French (1989) argue that expected returns are high in recessions and low in times of a booming economy. This discussion is enriched by the recent research of Bieri and Spremann (2009) and others who suggest a premia for taking cyclical risks. The previous view of one risk premium might be extended to a view with several risk premia. For instance, there may be a market risk premium which is the reward for taking exposure to the daily movements of the market portfolio. In addition, there could be a risk premium which compensates for exposure to macroeconomic fluctuations. If expected returns really do vary over time because of time-varying risk premia, it could be due to variation in the market risk premium or due to variation of the cyclical risk premium. With such a view in mind, stock prices are low in recessions and high during boom times because of their exposure to cyclical risks such as a recession and not because of the stock's exposure to market fluctuations. There might be only a small group of investors who is willing or able to hold stocks in a recession. Moreover, there may be market segments which most investors avoid even more in a recession. Cochrane (1999a; 2005a, p. 451) argues that small caps and value stocks fall into this category. This argument is supported for small caps by the research of Perez-Quiros and Timmermann (2000). In order to motivate some investors during a recession to hold assets like small caps and value stocks, there has to be a high expected return (Cochrane (1999a)). But the expected return is high in recessions because of the high risk premium for taking cyclical risks and not because of exposure to daily index fluctuations. In contrast, the expected return during boom times is low because of the low risk premium for taking cyclical risks. The next section uses an individual investor's perspective in order to shed more light on this kind of predictability. However, the presence of a time-varying risk premium for cyclical risks does not necessarily mean that the market risk premium is irrelevant or constant.

3.3.3. Investors and Return Predictability

As previously outlined, Boudoukh, Richardson, and Whitelaw (1994) identify market frictions, time-varying risk premia, and delayed reaction to new information as possible reasons for the ability of past returns to predict contemporaneous returns. The present section seeks to link these sources of predictability to an individual investor's situation. This may help to clarify the above explanations.

Suppose returns were predictable. If we were to assume that returns were predictable, it would be natural to question why not every investor exploited that predictability. The question is strongly linked to the previous section. It is important to know why returns might be predictable.

In the case of market frictions, predictability appears because of the way real world markets work and data is treated and stored. For instance, if a researcher accounts for bid/ask spreads or nonsynchronous trading, he does not find any predictability. Investors might be able to detect market frictions and account for them before entering into transactions. Hence, there would be nothing to exploit.

If return predictability arises from market inefficiencies forecasting is basically beneficial to every investor. Every investor who identifies mispricing could maximise his utility by exploiting the opportunity. However, the more investors exploit the opportunities, the less predictability is left. Thus, it might be the case that predictability would vanish after the detection of the market inefficiency.

In a world with return predictability because of changing prices of risks, it is different. The average investor should hold the market portfolio. The identifying characteristic regarding whether an investor is average or not is his risk profile. An example might be a setting with investors facing different exposures to recession risk. An investor with a very high exposure to declining business activity might find it useful to abstain from holding stocks in a recession despite high expected returns. For example, the investor might be the owner of a manufacturing company of electronic equipment. In a recession new orders might be low and the investor's ability to take cyclical risks may be close to non-existent. But who will hold stocks in a recession? It may be investors with a very low exposure to recession risk or people whose situation improves during a recession. For a more detailed treatment of these aspects I refer the interested reader to Cochrane (1999b), and Spremann (2007, pp. 467-486).

As the above explanation indicates, the detection of a working forecasting model can also be of interest in order to obtain more insight into how financial markets work. In other words, a working forecasting model might reveal market inefficiencies as well as new insights with respect to time-varying risk premia or market frictions. Moreover, depending on the reason for its forecasting power a given model should not be used by every single investor. The forecasting-based investment strategies presented in Chapter 7 will hopefully contribute to this discussion.

3.4. Style Investing

3.4.1. Approaches for the Allocation of Funds

Style investing is the second part of the foundation of my research. Unfortunately, the definition of style in the world of finance is not clear cut. Some authors call market timing, stock picking, cyclical investments, or long-short strategies styles. Other authors refer to style if an investment strategy is based on stocks which share a common characteristic such as a low book-to-market ratio. In the course of this dissertation, style investing plays a vital role. For instance, the classification into asset classes and the decision on how to allocate funds across these classes is at the heart of Chapter 7. Such an allocation process can be referred to as style investing (Barberis and Shleifer (2003)). However, other elements of style investing also exist: for example, investing on the basis of a forecasting model might also be an investment style. In other words, applying a forecasting model may lead to a conclusion regarding which asset classes should be bought or sold at a certain point in time. For instance, a portfolio manager might want to know whether value stocks or growth stocks should be held. This decision can be a part of the investment style cyclical investments or market timing. A broad interpretation of style investing might be that it is a systematic approach to determining tactical asset allocation. A concise description of style investing can be found in Spremann (2006, pp. 37-60).

3.4.2. Reasons for Emerging and Vanishing Styles

Barberis and Shleifer (2003) identify two reasons why new styles emerge. First, financial innovation can lead to new styles. For example, new asset classes such as mortgage-backed securities enable new styles. Second, a relatively good performance of a group sharing a common characteristic can lead to a new style. Two examples might be small caps and value stocks. After Banz (1981) and Reinganum (1981) discovered the small firm effect, many investment funds started following style investing with small caps. A similar evolution is true for value stocks. Today, modern financial instruments such as Exchange Traded Funds (ETF) allow participation in style investing for almost every investor. Moreover, the time to market for such instruments is short. If certain styles are profitable because of market inefficiencies, these inefficiencies will be exploited and should vanish. In contrast, if a style is profitable because of an exposure to a certain risk, it is likely to remain profitable.[7] According to Barberis and Shleifer (2003), a major reason why styles vanish is a poor performance of the respective style. As investors observe the underperformance for a while, the style is no longer able to attract new funds and existing funds flow into other styles.

[7] I take up the profitability of investment strategies again in the section on performance measurement.

3.4.3. Reasons for Following Style Investing

The grouping of individual securities in groups simplifies problems of choice. It might be easier to allocate funds to ten different styles than to thousands of individual securities. Simplification enables investors to process information more efficiently; hence, the simplification aspect can be one reason why investors prefer style investing over stock picking (Mullainathan (2002); Barberis and Shleifer (2003)). Another reason why investors choose to invest in styles is performance evaluation. According to Sharpe (1992), a style is likely to be followed by more than one asset manager. Thus, there is a peer group which enables comparisons of managers within a certain style. Moreover, a frequently followed style might be an impetus for the creation of indices which track the style, which in turn, reveals additional possibilities for evaluation such as exposure and alpha calculations.

3.4.4. Risks and Reward of Style-Based Investment Strategies

An investor who considers investing in a certain style might have two questions. The first one is whether a particular style works or not; the investor may be interested in the risk and return of a style. Second, the investor might wonder why the particular style works and what the sources of the profits are.

Both questions are related to findings discussed in the literature review. Fama and French (1993) show styles which outperform others. For instance, value stocks outperform growth stocks and small caps outperform large caps. Lakonishok, Shleifer, and Vishny (1994) attribute the higher return of value stocks over growth stocks to the suboptimal behaviour of the typical investor. However, as pointed out above, the outperformance might be due to risks not captured by Modern Portfolio Theory, in which risk is one dimensional. The possibility of exposure to cyclical risks may be an explanation for the outperformance of one style over another. Hence, with the possibility of multi dimensional risk in mind, style investing may be compared to selling insurance. Like an insurance company, a style investor takes specific risks and receives a reward in the form of a risk premium.

However, there are other risks an investor faces as he follows a style-based investment strategy. For example, a portfolio manager might decide to change his investment style over time, which may affect the risk characteristics of the portfolio. Thus, it is important to an investor to know whether a portfolio manager has been following the designated style and whether the style delivers a superior performance after accounting for other risks besides market exposure. These questions have been addressed by a number of researchers.

Brown and Goetzmann (1997) find several mutual funds which changed their investment objective ex post. Hence, a characteristics-based benchmark approach seems appealing. Daniel, Grinblatt, Titman, and Wermers (1997) provide an example of such an approach. Another approach is the application of multifactor benchmarks, as applied by Carhart (1997). Kothari and Warner (2001) find only modest differences between the two approaches, and thus, I do not go into more detail with respect to this discussion. Davis (2001) investigates whether particular investment styles deliver abnormal returns and whether performance persistence can be identified. On the basis of US data ranging from 1965 to 1998, Davis (2001) does not observe abnormal returns if the Fama-French factors are applied. Moreover, persistence can only be found in the returns of growth stocks and only for horizons up to one year. Chan, Chen, and Lakonishok (2002) find that growth managers do a better job than the managers of value funds. On average, growth managers outperform value managers by 1.2% per year if a four-factor model is applied which accounts for the Fama-French factors plus a momentum factor.

Besides following a particular style, there is the possibility of rotating among different styles based on a pre-specified methodology. Such style rotation strategies require a forecasting model. Arshanapalli, Switzer, and Panju (2007) apply a multinomial timing model in order to switch across large cap growth, large cap value, small cap growth, and small cap value stocks. They find a significant outperformance with respect to risk-adjusted returns. Moreover, the applied strategy earned considerably higher returns than a buy and hold investment in the best performing style index. Swinkels and Tjong-A-Tjoe (2007) investigate the style timing ability of mutual fund managers. Their research shows that fund managers have timing skills in value and momentum styles. In contrast, their results do not indicate superior timing abilities with respect to switches between large caps and small caps.

4. Study Design and Data

4.1. Research Methodology

In order to answer the research questions, the starting point is the construction of the six Fama-French Portfolios, which range from small value stocks to large growth stocks. These portfolios also serve as a basis for the calculation of the returns of the factor-mimicking portfolios SMB and HML.

The empirical study consists of two parts. Each part is intended to reject or accept one of the hypotheses stated at the beginning of the respective chapter. The first part tests whether the returns of various (style) portfolios might be predictable to some extent. These analyses are based on tests of the random walk model. The second part evaluates whether investment strategies which exploit lead-lag predictability can beat the market or not.

In order to being able to test for predictability of factor-mimicking portfolios or their components and to reject or accept the hypotheses, I follow several process steps. In a first step, I gather sample data from reliable databases. This data is then analysed and checked for inconsistencies. Based on a sorted data set, I construct the six Fama-French Portfolios as well as the two factor-mimicking portfolios SMB and HML. In addition, a proxy, called MKT, for the market portfolio is constructed. This portfolio primarily serves as a benchmark and as a factor which covers the market risk. Moreover, MKT is useful in checking for the data quality as its returns are intended to mimic the returns of the Swiss Performance Index, which serves as the investment universe. Thereafter, the Random Walk Hypothesis is tested. I apply two tests, the first of which is based on autocorrelation coefficients. The second test applies variance ratios and also accounts for possible heteroskedasticity. Both test procedures are described in more detail below.

Step	Action	Chapter
1	Gather sample data	4
2	Analyse data and check for inconsistencies	4
3	Construct Fama-French Portfolios and Factors	4
4	Test Random Walk Hypothesis for portfolios	5
5	Build forecasting models	6
6	Create and evaluate investment strategies	7

Table 1: Research process
Table 1 summarises the six steps which are conducted to answer the research questions. The steps are covered in four subsequent chapters.

Table 1 summarises the steps of the applied research process. The findings of the random walk tests and the empirical results on lead-lag relationships which are documented in the literature serve as the basis for the construction of forecasting models. In turn, these forecasting models are applied in order to create investment strategies. The performance of these investment strategies is then evaluated by well-known performance measures as well as more recent approaches. The applied performance evaluations are described in a separate section.

4.2. Data

The construction of the Fama-French Portfolios requires various data and I focus a great deal of attention on the accuracy of the data. However, to my knowledge, long-time series of the required Swiss data are not readily available and only a few databases seem to provide reasonable data. Hence, some restrictions might apply when comparing results across different studies.

In order to build the time series of SMB and HML, one needs the market capitalisation, the book-to-market ratio or the price-to-book ratio, dividend information, and price histories of the stock universe under consideration. The universe for the Swiss data set consists of the members of the Swiss Performance

Index (SPI). For these stocks, price information and market capitalisation were obtained directly from the SIX Swiss Exchange. The price-to-book ratio and the dividend information were retrieved from the database "Factset". However, missing data was also checked with the database "Datastream" and filled in if available. Datastream is also the source for the one-month Swiss Franc LIBOR, which serves as a proxy for the risk-free rate and is used to calculate excess returns. Due to changes in company names and ISINs over time and different data sources, a matching procedure including visits of company websites was conducted.

The data gathering procedure allowed the construction of time series with a length of 180 monthly observations, i.e., the data covers 15 years of returns history, ranging from July 1993 to June 2008. In order to check for time-varying characteristics, the full sample period was split into three subsample periods of 60-months' length each. The first subperiod ranges from July 1993 to June 1998, the second subperiod covers data from July 1998 to June 2003, and the third subsample period contains data of the time period July 2003 to June 2008.

4.3. Construction of Fama-French Portfolios

The factors SMB and HML are returns of long-short portfolios. SMB means Small Minus Big and HML is an abbreviation for High Minus Low. Small and Big refer to the market capitalisation, while High and Low are measured by the book-to-market ratio. Hence, the return of SMB in a month t is the return differential between small caps and large caps. The return of HML in a month t is the return differential between value stocks and growth stocks. Fama and French (1992; 1993) use a universe consisting of the stocks listed at one of the exchanges NYSE, Amex, or Nasdaq. However, Fama and French (1992; 1993) do not determine the four portfolios Small, Big, High, and Low directly. They start with six intersectional portfolios called SH, SM, SL, BH, BM, BL. For example, the portfolio SH consists of stocks which are small and have a high book-to-market ratio. The portfolio BL consists of stocks which are big, measured by market capitalisation, and have a low book-to-market ratio. In order to build these portfolios Fama and French (1992; 1993) rank their stocks each June, once according to the market capitalisation and once according to the book-to-market ratio. The median of the NYSE-stocks is used to split the universe into small caps and large caps. The 30th and 70th percentile of the NYSE-stocks is used to split the companies into a group of value stocks and a group of growth stocks.[8] The medium forty percent are represented by the letter M in SM and BM. A stock which has an above-median market capitalisation and belongs to the thirty percent with the highest book-to-market ratio is therefore a large value stock and a member of the BH-portfolio. Finally, each stock belongs to one of the six portfolios. As the rankings and portfolio formations are repeated each June, the portfolio components as well as the number of stocks in each portfolio will change over time. However, this procedure ensures that the criteria small, big, value, and growth determine the portfolios' returns. After constructing each of the six portfolios, their monthly value-weighted returns are calculated. The value-weighted returns of SH, SM, SL, BH, BM, and BL are then used to calculate the returns of SMB and HML.

(7) $$SMB_t = \frac{1}{3} \cdot (SH_t + SM_t + SL_t) - \frac{1}{3} \cdot (BH_t + BM_t + BL_t)$$

(8) $$HML_t = \frac{1}{2} \cdot (SH_t + BH_t) - \frac{1}{2} \cdot (SL_t + BL_t)$$

The formulas above show how the SMB and HML returns are obtained. The return of SMB in a month t is the arithmetic average of the returns of the small cap portfolios minus the arithmetic average of the returns of the large cap portfolios. The return of HML in a month t is calculated in a similar way. However, HML does not use the medium portfolios, which consist of stocks which are neither value stocks nor growth stocks. The factor MKT is constructed from the weighted returns of all stocks belonging to one of the six Fama-French Portfolios.

[8] Value stocks have a high book-to-market ratio and growth stocks have a low book-to-market ratio.

I follow the construction approach of Fama and French (1993). However, there are some differences. The first is the treatment of financials. Fama and French (1993) exclude all financials; however, this might be inappropriate for the Swiss market. Financials have a large share of the entire market capitalisation and are one of the main drivers of the Swiss economy. Another difference is the utilisation of the price-to-book ratio instead of the book-to-market ratio. This was decided because of the better availability of the price-to-book ratio. The third difference is related to the price-to-book ratio. The ranking is conducted with the June-values of the price-to-book ratios, i.e., the share price in June is put into relation to the last available book value, which does not necessarily have to be the December-value. Fama and French (1993) use the book values of year end at $t-1$ and the share price of June at year t.

4.4. Descriptive Statistics

As mentioned above, in order to construct the Fama-French Factors, the six portfolios SH,...,BL have to be put in place. The investment universe is the Swiss Performance Index, i.e., the constituents of that index. However, because of limited data availability it was not possible to include each stock at each point in time. Hence, MKT will deviate from the SPI. The table below illustrates the impact of the deviations.

	MKT		SPI		
	Mean	Std. Deviation	Mean	Std. Deviation	Correlation
Jul1993-Jun2008	8.65%	15.23%	9.11%	16.13%	0.97
Jul1993-Jun1998	22.73%	14.90%	23.89%	14.54%	0.91
Jul1998-Jun2003	-7.21%	17.56%	-7.22%	20.04%	0.99
Jul2003-Jun2008	10.43%	11.62%	10.65%	11.61%	1.00

Table 2: Annualised data for MKT and the Swiss Performance Index
The above table shows annualised mean returns and standard deviations for the constructed index MKT and the Swiss Performance Index SPI. The analysis is based on monthly continuously compounded returns. The full sample period (first line) is divided into three subsamples (subsequent lines).

The data above confirm the close relationship between MKT and the SPI, with differences occurring mainly in the first subsample period. Increasing data availability leaves almost no differences in the first two moments of the index returns. Because of the close relationship between the two indices, I will focus on MKT in subsequent analyses.

	1993	1994	1995	1996	1997	1998	1999	2000	2001	2002	2003	2004	2005	2006	2007
						Panel A: Number of companies in each portfolio									
MKT	60	63	98	107	122	151	164	189	226	200	191	197	193	212	215
BL	10	14	20	20	24	32	36	44	53	50	43	44	42	46	48
BM	14	11	21	26	28	31	33	41	43	38	39	41	37	42	42
BH	6	6	8	8	9	13	13	10	17	12	14	14	18	18	18
SL	8	5	9	12	13	13	13	13	15	10	15	15	16	18	17
SM	10	14	19	17	20	30	33	34	47	42	37	38	40	42	43
SH	12	13	21	24	28	32	36	47	51	48	43	45	40	46	47
						Panel B: Market Cap in CHF Mio. (mean)									
MKT	1,838	2,026	2,054	2,214	2,419	4,721	4,125	5,248	4,094	3,824	3,288	3,844	4,392	4,936	6,066
BL	10,077	8,325	8,022	9,353	10,119	19,678	16,607	16,578	12,905	12,921	12,373	13,079	15,147	16,736	11,617
BM	452	708	1,647	1,526	941	2,020	1,737	5,542	4,975	2,839	2,203	3,894	4,765	5,704	15,365
BH	329	243	322	669	526	938	998	2,185	886	450	615	1,069	1,398	1,288	4,579
SL	36	56	92	128	135	159	106	218	136	41	55	83	125	182	187
SM	54	58	74	88	89	109	115	128	108	61	51	79	113	137	228
SH	32	58	71	76	77	93	89	131	100	50	44	66	87	103	126
						Panel C: Price-to-Book Ratio (mean)									
MKT	1.33	1.89	1.93	2.25	2.54	3.27	4.34	3.97	2.54	2.09	1.72	2.66	2.89	2.66	3.79
BL	2.65	4.43	4.54	5.94	6.00	7.29	7.51	10.74	5.78	4.54	4.07	6.63	7.33	5.30	7.61
BM	1.05	1.23	1.21	1.31	1.62	2.10	1.73	2.04	1.69	1.35	1.14	1.55	1.67	1.94	2.63
BH	0.48	0.61	0.62	0.76	0.72	1.03	0.76	0.96	0.62	0.69	0.63	0.86	1.01	1.16	1.30
SL	2.52	3.18	3.83	3.88	4.90	7.32	22.47	6.63	5.42	5.05	2.68	4.48	4.33	4.77	6.76
SM	1.03	1.25	1.25	1.29	1.49	2.07	1.70	1.88	1.51	1.30	1.11	1.50	1.69	2.01	2.59
SH	0.45	0.49	0.48	0.56	0.68	0.76	0.70	0.75	0.66	0.55	0.47	0.70	0.84	1.03	1.25

Table 3: Number of companies, market capitalisation, and price-to-book ratios
Panel A shows the number of companies allocated to each portfolio during the sample period. Panel B identifies the average market capitalisation of the companies per portfolio. The average is the arithmetic mean of the market capitalisation. Panel C shows the average price-to-book ratio for each portfolio. The observations were taken at the end of June of the respective year.

The table above represents information about the number of companies, the market capitalisation, and the price-to-book ratios of the six Fama-French Portfolios SH,...,BL plus the aggregate market MKT. In particular, the table shows the development of these figures throughout the sample period. Vaihekoski (2004) suggests that the number of companies in a portfolio should not be less than five. This lower bound is hit only once during the entire sample period. The data availability increased in the more recent past, and thus, an increasing number of companies could be included in the sample through time. The panel containing the average market capitalisation represents the expected result. Portfolios consisting of large caps show a higher average market capitalisation than small cap portfolios, and growth stocks usually have a higher average market capitalisation than value stocks. Another analysis, which is not reported, shows a much higher mean market capitalisation than median market capitalisation. This highlights a special characteristic of the Swiss stock market: A few stocks represent the majority of the market capitalisation. For the entire sample period, on average, the mean is approximately sixteen times higher than the median. The price-to-book ratios reveal some valuation insights. Overall the price-to-book ratio seems to be higher for large caps than for small caps; however, this relationship seems to be most consistent for value stocks. Except for 2001, large value stocks show a higher ratio than small value stocks. Roughly speaking, it seems to make a difference whether a company is large and distressed or small and distressed.

In order to give a more comprehensive picture on the data, additional analyses are conducted. Note that I use risk premia in the following statistics as the models will also be based on risk premia (excess returns).[9]

[9] If not stated otherwise, the additional term _RF refers to the use of excess returns.

	Jul1993-Jun2008	Jul1993-Jun1998	Jul1998-Jun2003	Jul2003-Jun2008
		Panel A: Average Risk Premium		
SH_RF	13.32%	16.19%	0.74%	23.01%
SM_RF	10.92%	15.93%	-5.18%	22.01%
SL_RF	11.24%	16.33%	-9.37%	26.75%
BH_RF	11.06%	21.19%	-1.09%	13.08%
BM_RF	4.38%	17.06%	-14.86%	10.95%
BL_RF	7.10%	20.25%	-8.45%	9.49%
SMALL_RF	12.24%	16.43%	-3.79%	24.10%
BIG_RF	7.95%	19.88%	-7.51%	11.47%
VALUE_RF	12.55%	19.03%	0.31%	18.30%
GROWTH_RF	9.62%	18.54%	-8.10%	18.42%
SMB	3.73%	-3.92%	2.64%	12.46%
HML	1.98%	-0.27%	6.52%	-0.32%
MKT_RF	6.74%	20.08%	-9.02%	9.16%
		Panel B: Std. Deviation		
SH_RF	14.52%	15.09%	14.97%	12.87%
SM_RF	16.14%	13.87%	18.78%	14.51%
SL_RF	22.95%	15.28%	31.50%	17.71%
BH_RF	18.39%	14.82%	21.39%	18.09%
BM_RF	21.83%	15.24%	30.28%	15.73%
BL_RF	14.94%	15.90%	16.47%	10.85%
SMALL_RF	15.67%	12.73%	18.78%	13.97%
BIG_RF	16.07%	12.54%	20.54%	13.08%
VALUE_RF	14.26%	12.51%	15.67%	14.00%
GROWTH_RF	16.75%	13.89%	21.40%	12.67%
SMB	10.48%	9.35%	12.24%	9.20%
HML	11.03%	10.91%	13.02%	8.85%
MKT_RF	15.28%	15.00%	17.58%	11.72%
		Panel C: Sharpe Ratio		
SH_RF	0.92	1.07	0.05	1.79
SM_RF	0.68	1.15	-0.28	1.52
SL_RF	0.49	1.07	-0.30	1.51
BH_RF	0.60	1.43	-0.05	0.72
BM_RF	0.20	1.12	-0.49	0.70
BL_RF	0.48	1.27	-0.51	0.87
SMALL_RF	0.78	1.29	-0.20	1.72
BIG_RF	0.49	1.59	-0.37	0.88
VALUE_RF	0.88	1.52	0.02	1.31
GROWTH_RF	0.57	1.33	-0.38	1.45
SMB	0.36	-0.42	0.22	1.35
HML	0.18	-0.02	0.50	-0.04
MKT_RF	0.44	1.34	-0.51	0.78

Table 4: Risk premia, standard deviations, and Sharpe Ratios
The above table shows annualised data for the six Fama-French Portfolios, SMB and HML, as well as for MKT. Note that _RF indicates the utilisation of excess returns. For SMB and HML, returns are close to excess returns as these returns are calculated from long-short portfolios. Panel A shows the risk premia, Panel B the standard deviations and Panel C the respective Sharpe Ratios. The calculations are based on monthly data. As SMB and HML are logs of a return and SMALL_RF, BIG_RF, VALUE_RF, and GROWTH_RF are also the logs of returns, it is not possible to construct SMB and HML from SMALL_RF, BIG_RF, VALUE_RF, and GROWTH_RF.

Panel A presents the risk premia of the six Fama-French Portfolios, SMB, HML, and MKT. Additionally, the risk premia of the four portfolios SMALL, BIG, VALUE, and GROWTH are presented. The returns of these portfolios are calculated by using equations 7 and 8. As can be seen, the portfolio consisting of small value stocks has the highest risk premia over the entire sample period. This is in line with the findings of Banz (1981) and Reinganum (1981), who report higher average returns of small caps over large caps. Cochrane (2005a, p. 452) reports a decline of the small cap effect after its publication. In contrast, Reinganum (1992) documents persistence of the small cap effect. The above data supports this finding. Small caps outperformed large caps in the most recent past of the sample period.

Small value stocks did especially well from 1998 until 2003. Moreover, SH and VALUE are the only portfolios with positive risk premia across all three subsample periods. However, there are other long-only portfolios which exhibit higher returns than SH or VALUE in the first and last subsample period. The two factor-mimicking portfolios, SMB and HML, also carry positive risk premia. The premia are somewhat different to those presented by Ammann and Steiner (2008). However, this is reasonable because of a slightly different calculation methodology and a different sample period. In overlapping subperiods the sign of the premia seems consistent. Panel B, which represents the standard deviations of the above-mentioned portfolios, allows additional insights. It seems that there is only a very weak link between risk premia and their standard deviations. For instance, the portfolio BM had a very low average risk premium but an exceptionally high standard deviation. In particular, the standard deviation was high in the period when the average risk premium was negative. The Sharpe Ratios in Panel C confirm this finding. The highest excess return per unit of standard deviation can be found in the small value stocks. Again, this is not true for the subsample periods.

	SH	SM	SL	BH	BM	BL	MKT
1993	31.72%	17.94%	24.03%	25.37%	18.49%	20.78%	20.69%
1994	12.10%	3.69%	-10.26%	-10.57%	0.75%	-0.92%	-0.82%
1995	-3.69%	-3.49%	9.79%	1.59%	-1.24%	21.22%	18.83%
1996	10.04%	20.77%	11.79%	16.97%	16.04%	11.04%	12.01%
1997	25.13%	27.46%	31.58%	56.96%	28.42%	41.25%	40.28%
1998	13.81%	12.11%	3.16%	1.97%	12.43%	16.96%	16.46%
1999	16.94%	35.65%	42.72%	17.01%	7.94%	6.25%	6.77%
2000	6.55%	4.95%	40.82%	38.42%	22.93%	6.98%	9.95%
2001	5.96%	-35.42%	-27.23%	-37.62%	-21.17%	-22.44%	-22.02%
2002	-13.14%	-14.31%	-91.67%	2.21%	-54.92%	-23.42%	-28.40%
2003	28.70%	31.22%	55.06%	45.31%	17.83%	17.63%	18.26%
2004	33.64%	20.85%	21.68%	4.10%	11.18%	5.61%	6.66%
2005	28.01%	30.75%	26.12%	33.81%	31.88%	29.87%	30.41%
2006	27.74%	30.37%	39.53%	23.57%	23.80%	15.33%	17.73%
2007	12.12%	17.34%	34.71%	-16.76%	4.34%	-0.90%	-0.34%
2008	-7.40%	-7.39%	-14.69%	-7.77%	-24.22%	-10.14%	-16.72%
Min	-13.14%	-35.42%	-91.67%	-37.62%	-54.92%	-23.42%	-28.40%
Max	33.64%	35.65%	55.06%	56.96%	31.88%	41.25%	40.28%

Table 5: Annual returns
Table 5 represents annualised returns of the six Fama-French Portfolios and the market. Note that the returns from the years 1993 and 2008 cover only six months instead of a full calendar year. The returns are calculated as sums of the monthly log-returns.

The above representation by calendar year is intended to enable a closer look at the behaviour of the returns of the Fama-French Portfolios in various economic situations. For instance, between 1997 and 2000, the time of the tech rally, strong returns of SL can be observed, while the other growth portfolio, BL, evolves in line with the market. However, market participants seem to differentiate among size as well as among valuation. In 2001 all portfolios except SH show a negative return. Moreover, in 2002 small growth stocks do extremely poorly, while small value stocks beat the market. Similar observations can be made for large caps. However, I do not investigate how the returns of the different portfolios are generated. A detailed analysis with US data of migration and other characteristics which influence the performance of the portfolios can be found in Fama and French (2007a; 2007b).

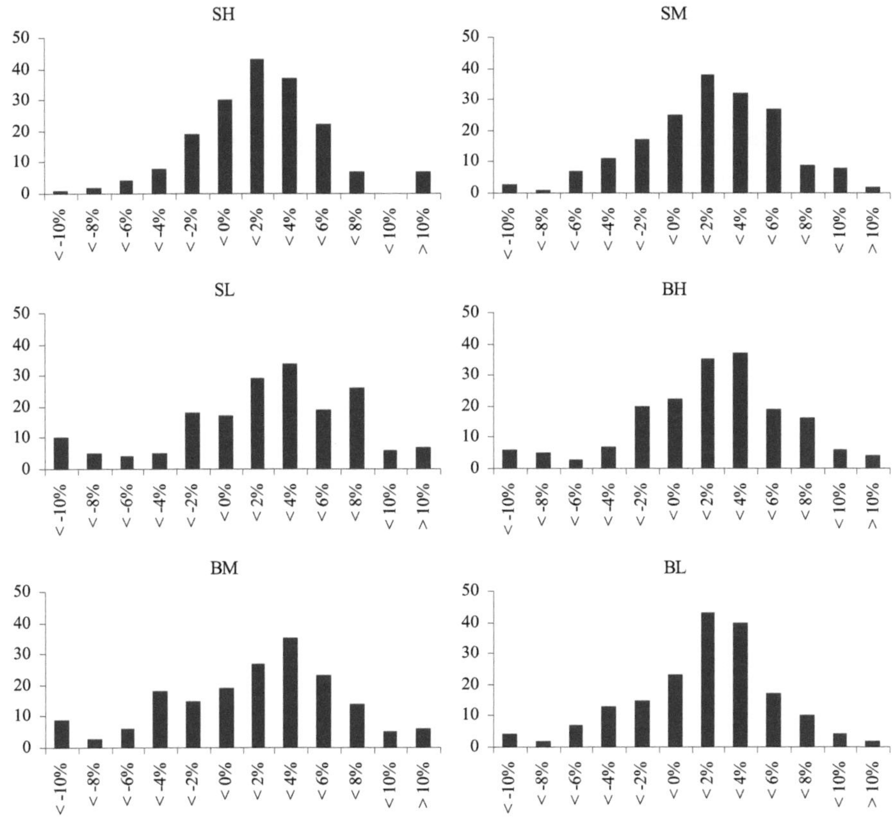

Figure 1: Return distributions of the six Fama-French Portfolios
Figure 1 illustrates the return distributions of the portfolios SH,...,BL. The X-axis refers to the magnitude of the returns. The Y-axis refers to the number of observations. For example, more than 40 return observations of the SH-Portfolio are between 0% and 2%. The data covers the returns between Jul1993 and Jun2008, i.e., 180 observations.

Overall, the above figure seems to support the evidence on fat tails in returns, which were first described by Mandelbrot (1963). Unreported Jarque-Bera test statistics indicate a rejection of the hypothesis of a normal distribution at the 1% level for SH and SL, at the 5% level for BH, and at the 10% level for SM and BM. The hypothesis of a normal distribution for BL cannot be rejected at the 10% level.[10] With respect to

[10] In order to account for extreme values which might be due to data irregularities, the sample for the test was restricted to returns between -15% and +15%.

extreme observations, additional remarks might be of interest. First, SH is the only portfolio which shows more values greater than 10% than negative values less than -10%. Furthermore, all portfolios show more returns greater than 6% than returns less than -6%. Moreover, the returns of the small growth stocks are the farthest away from a normal distribution, while the returns of the large growth stocks are the ones closest to a normal distribution. Hence, it seems that capitalisation is more relevant than valuation with respect to return distribution.

	BH_RF	BM_RF	BL_RF	SH_RF	SM_RF	SL_RF	SPI_RF	MKT_RF	BIG_RF	SML_RF	VAL_RF	GRO_RF	SMB	HML
BH_RF	1.00													
BM_RF	0.65	1.00												
BL_RF	0.56	0.72	1.00											
SH_RF	0.49	0.58	0.56	1.00										
SM_RF	0.63	0.70	0.57	0.67	1.00									
SL_RF	0.59	0.70	0.56	0.59	0.71	1.00								
SPI_RF	0.66	0.85	0.94	0.58	0.66	0.65	1.00							
MKT_RF	0.63	0.82	0.98	0.60	0.64	0.63	0.97	1.00						
BIG_RF	0.85	0.92	0.85	0.62	0.73	0.71	0.92	0.91	1.00					
SMALL_RF	0.65	0.75	0.64	0.83	0.89	0.91	0.72	0.71	0.78	1.00				
VALUE_RF	0.89	0.71	0.65	0.83	0.75	0.68	0.72	0.71	0.86	0.84	1.00			
GROWTH_RF	0.65	0.80	0.83	0.65	0.74	0.93	0.86	0.86	0.86	0.90	0.75	1.00		
SMB	-0.32	-0.28	-0.34	0.30	0.23	0.27	-0.33	-0.34	-0.35	0.30	-0.05	0.04	1.00	
HML	0.19	-0.27	-0.40	0.10	-0.14	-0.50	-0.36	-0.36	-0.17	-0.26	0.18	-0.52	-0.12	1.00

Table 6: Correlation coefficients – Jul1993-Jun2008
The table above shows the correlation coefficients of the six Fama-French Portfolios, MKT, SPI, BIG, SMALL, VALUE, GROWTH, SMB, and HML. The coefficients are based on monthly excess returns from Jul1993 to Jun2008.

A first look at the correlation coefficients provides additional information about the interrelations between the portfolios. The highest correlations among the six Fama-French Portfolios can be found between BL and BM, SM and BM, and SM and SL. However, in general, the correlations among the six Fama-French Portfolios are positive and of considerable magnitude. The highest correlation overall is between MKT and BL, which again shows the high impact of a few stocks on the market. The correlation between the two factors SMB and HML is slightly negative. The same is true for the correlation between MKT and the two Fama-French Factors. However, it might be interesting to have information on the change of correlations across time.

	BH_RF	BM_RF	BL_RF	SH_RF	SM_RF	SL_RF	SPI_RF	MKT_RF	BIG_RF	SML_RF	VAL_RF	GRO_RF	SMB	HML
BH_RF	1.00													
BM_RF	0.45	1.00												
BL_RF	0.46	0.60	1.00											
SH_RF	0.39	0.50	0.55	1.00										
SM_RF	0.46	0.68	0.60	0.64	1.00									
SL_RF	0.39	0.55	0.59	0.56	0.66	1.00								
SPI_RF	0.52	0.69	0.90	0.52	0.65	0.60	1.00							
MKT_RF	0.49	0.68	0.99	0.57	0.63	0.60	0.91	1.00						
BIG_RF	0.77	0.84	0.85	0.59	0.71	0.62	0.86	0.88	1.00					
SMALL_RF	0.48	0.66	0.67	0.85	0.88	0.86	0.68	0.69	0.74	1.00				
VALUE_RF	0.83	0.57	0.61	0.84	0.65	0.57	0.63	0.63	0.82	0.80	1.00			
GROWTH_RF	0.48	0.64	0.89	0.63	0.70	0.89	0.85	0.90	0.83	0.86	0.66	1.00		
SMB	-0.41	-0.22	-0.23	0.37	0.25	0.34	-0.23	-0.24	-0.35	0.38	-0.02	0.06	1.00	
HML	0.35	-0.16	-0.43	0.16	-0.15	-0.47	-0.35	-0.41	-0.10	-0.18	0.31	-0.51	-0.11	1.00

Table 7: Correlation coefficients – Jul1993-Jun1998
The table above shows the correlation coefficients of the six Fama-French Portfolios, MKT, SPI, BIG, SMALL, VALUE, GROWTH, SMB, and HML. The coefficients are based on monthly excess returns from Jul1993 to Jun1998.

Table 7 focuses on the correlation coefficients of the first subperiod. Comparing the coefficients of the first subperiod to the coefficients of the full sample period does not reveal dramatic differences in the relationships. However, the correlation coefficients tend to be somewhat lower in the first subperiod than in the full sample. As the column marked BH_RF indicates, the most considerable differences seem to be in relationships where large value stocks are involved.

	BH_RF	BM_RF	BL_RF	SH_RF	SM_RF	SL_RF	SPI_RF	MKT_RF	BIG_RF	SML_RF	VAL_RF	GRO_RF	SMB	HML
BH_RF	1.00													
BM_RF	0.71	1.00												
BL_RF	0.64	0.80	1.00											
SH_RF	0.46	0.61	0.52	1.00										
SM_RF	0.68	0.72	0.53	0.57	1.00									
SL_RF	0.64	0.75	0.58	0.56	0.68	1.00								
SPI_RF	0.72	0.90	0.97	0.56	0.64	0.68	1.00							
MKT_RF	0.69	0.88	0.98	0.57	0.60	0.64	0.99	1.00						
BIG_RF	0.87	0.95	0.88	0.59	0.73	0.74	0.95	0.94	1.00					
SMALL_RF	0.70	0.81	0.63	0.77	0.86	0.92	0.74	0.71	0.81	1.00				
VALUE_RF	0.90	0.77	0.69	0.80	0.73	0.70	0.76	0.74	0.87	0.85	1.00			
GROWTH_RF	0.72	0.85	0.81	0.61	0.70	0.95	0.86	0.85	0.88	0.92	0.78	1.00		
SMB	-0.31	-0.34	-0.49	0.20	0.12	0.17	-0.45	-0.47	-0.42	0.19	-0.14	-0.06	1.00	
HML	-0.08	-0.44	-0.47	0.00	-0.26	-0.66	-0.48	-0.47	-0.37	-0.45	-0.05	-0.66	-0.06	1.00

Table 8: Correlation coefficients – Jul1998-Jun2003
The table above shows the correlation coefficients of the six Fama-French Portfolios, MKT, SPI, BIG, SMALL, VALUE, GROWTH, SMB, and HML. The coefficients are based on monthly excess returns from Jul1998 to Jun2003.

The correlation coefficients of the second subperiod are shown in Table 8. Comparing these coefficients to those of the first subperiod gives a mixed picture. Overall, the correlations seem to have become stronger. This effect is especially strong where big value stocks are involved. In other words, the correlation between big value stocks and other portfolios has increased from the first to the second subperiod. With respect to the full sample period, the correlation coefficients do not show considerable deviations.

	BH_RF	BM_RF	BL_RF	SH_RF	SM_RF	SL_RF	SPI_RF	MKT_RF	BIG_RF	SML_RF	VAL_RF	GRO_RF	SMB	HML
BH_RF	1.00													
BM_RF	0.69	1.00												
BL_RF	0.53	0.74	1.00											
SH_RF	0.63	0.66	0.62	1.00										
SM_RF	0.67	0.68	0.59	0.84	1.00									
SL_RF	0.62	0.63	0.55	0.74	0.81	1.00								
SPI_RF	0.68	0.90	0.94	0.69	0.70	0.65	1.00							
MKT_RF	0.68	0.90	0.94	0.69	0.69	0.65	1.00	1.00						
BIG_RF	0.88	0.92	0.82	0.72	0.74	0.69	0.93	0.93	1.00					
SMALL_RF	0.69	0.71	0.63	0.91	0.95	0.93	0.73	0.72	0.77	1.00				
VALUE_RF	0.93	0.75	0.62	0.87	0.82	0.74	0.75	0.75	0.90	0.86	1.00			
GROWTH_RF	0.66	0.76	0.81	0.78	0.82	0.93	0.86	0.85	0.83	0.92	0.78	1.00		
SMB	0.06	-0.24	-0.21	0.35	0.38	0.44	-0.21	-0.22	-0.25	0.43	0.03	0.22	1.00	
HML	0.55	0.11	-0.15	0.28	0.14	-0.15	-0.01	-0.01	0.25	0.07	0.48	-0.17	-0.25	1.00

Table 9: Correlation coefficients – Jul2003-Jun2008
The table above shows the correlation coefficients of the six Fama-French Portfolios, MKT, SPI, BIG, SMALL, VALUE, GROWTH, SMB, and HML. The coefficients are based on monthly excess returns from Jul2003 to Jun2008.

The most considerable changes in correlations occurred where HML was involved. As Table 9 shows, these correlations turned much less negative compared to the previous subperiod. A similar behaviour can be observed for returns of SMB. However, SMB seems to have stronger absolute correlations to other portfolios than HML. Except for SMB and HML, no other portfolio shows considerable changes in the correlation coefficients. The same is true for comparisons to the full sample period.

This section on descriptive statistics has revealed some interesting aspects such as changing correlations or risk premia of the combined style portfolios. In the following chapters these portfolios will be further analysed with respect to return predictability.

5. Empirical Part I – Testing for Predictability

5.1. Hypothesis I

The returns of the Fama-French factor-mimicking Portfolios or of components of these portfolios follow a random walk.

Chapter 5 presents tests of the above-stated hypothesis, which is derived from the research question formulated in the introduction. Besides the motivation outlined along the formulation of the first research question, there are additional factors which favour tests of predictability based on past returns. As shown in the literature review, there is an extensive number of potential forecasting variables and some of them seem to have promising forecasting power. However, each of them has its drawbacks. A major constraint for Swiss companies is data availability. There are almost no such long-time series available, as there are for US data, which makes it difficult to test certain variables since no sufficient sample can be gathered. This is especially true for the company level or for certain market segments. However, with respect to the effects of the real economy on return predictability, a market segment perspective seems important. Another challenge is the data frequency. Some variables such as accounting numbers are updated only one to four times a year. Additionally, historical practices contribute to a low data frequency. For instance, it is common for Swiss companies to pay dividends on an annual basis rather than each quarter. Moreover, some time series of the above-mentioned variables are difficult to handle econometrically. Testing the Random Walk Hypothesis might overcome some of the stated problems.

5.2. Autocorrelation Coefficients and Variance Ratios

There is a difference between the research question stated in the introduction and the hypothesis outlined above. The research question allows for cross-serial correlation, while the hypothesis focuses on autocorrelation. The reason is the so-called implied cross-autocorrelation, given in equation (9).

$$(9) \qquad corr(R_{it}, R_{jt-1}) = corr(R_{it}, R_{jt}) \cdot corr(R_{it}, R_{it-1})$$

Boudoukh, Richardson, and Whitelaw (1994) argue that cross-serial correlation $corr(R_{it}, R_{jt-1})$ between two portfolios i and j can be determined by a portfolio's own autocorrelation $corr(R_{it}, R_{it-1})$ and the contemporaneous correlation $corr(R_{it}, R_{jt})$ between the two portfolios. As the relationship between the contemporaneous correlation and the serial correlation is multiplicative a test of autocorrelation or contemporaneous correlation might be sufficient in order to answer the research question.

As Table 6 of the previous chapter indicates, there is considerable contemporaneous correlation among the portfolios. Thus, with the above formula in mind, a test of contemporaneous correlation does not seem promising. Moreover, it seems implausible to test for no contemporaneous correlation among stock returns as it is well documented in the literature. In contrast, testing whether the portfolios' returns follow a random walk may be a more appealing approach. Nevertheless, implied cross-autocorrelation might deviate from empirical cross-serial correlations. Therefore, in Chapter 6, with forecasting and investment strategies in view, I provide the empirical values and compare them to the results obtained by (9).

There are several approaches which may be applied in order to test for serial correlation. However, there might be more tests which can be applied to test RW1 than possible tests for RW2 or RW3. In the following, I will focus on one test for RW1 and one test which can be adjusted to test the RW3 model, which is the most general model. Hence, a rejection of RW3 would yield the strongest evidence against the Random Walk Hypothesis. Moreover, RW3 is the one most tested in the more recent literature.

Campbell, Lo, and MacKinlay (1997, pp. 33-55) provide various tests for the random walk hypotheses. An intuitive and direct approach is to test for serial correlation. Another test focuses on the linearity property of the variance. This property states that the variance of the increments of the random walk must be a linear function of the time interval. In the following, I briefly outline the two test procedures mentioned.

The first test checks for serial correlation in an individual time series. In the random walk model, log-returns should be uncorrelated at all leads and lags. Therefore, a direct approach is to test the null hypothesis that log-returns are uncorrelated at various leads and lags. Thus, the first step is to calculate the correlation coefficients. A theoretical description of the autocorrelation coefficient $\rho(k)$ is:

(10) $$\rho(k)=\frac{\sum_{t=k+1}^{T}((Y_t-\overline{Y})(Y_{t-k}-\overline{Y}_{t-k}))/(T-K)}{\sum_{t=1}^{T}(Y_t-\overline{Y})^2/T},$$

with $\overline{Y}_{t-k}=\sum Y_{t-k}/(T-k)$. However, the statistical package which is used for the tests below applies a slightly different estimator

(11) $$\rho(k)=\frac{\sum_{t=k+1}^{T}((Y_t-\overline{Y})(Y_{t-k}-\overline{Y}))}{\sum_{t=1}^{T}(Y_t-\overline{Y})^2}.$$

As can be seen from equations (10) and (11), the difference is with respect to the calculation of the sample means $\overline{Y}$ and $\overline{Y}_{t-k}$ of Y_t and Y_{t-k}, respectively. While the theoretical description is based on two different means, the statistics software applies the same overall sample mean $\overline{Y}$. This induces the results to be biased toward zero.

Under the assumption of standard normally distributed Y_t, the sample autocorrelation coefficients are also approximately normally distributed. Hence, significance tests for the autocorrelation coefficients can be conducted. The significance test requires the construction of a confidence interval. For example, the 5% significance level is given by

$$\pm 1.96 \cdot \frac{1}{\sqrt{T}}.$$

The above test is restricted to a single lag-structure. In contrast, the Q-statistic, based on the work of Box and Pierce (1970), allows for a joint test that there is no autocorrelation up to order k. The Q-statistic is given by

$$(12) \qquad Q = T \sum_{k=1}^{m} \rho^2(k),$$

with sample size T and maximum lag length m. The Q-statistic is asymptotically distributed as χ_K^2, with null hypothesis that all m autocorrelation coefficients are zero. However, this statistic has a poor performance in small samples. Thus, Ljung and Box (1978) suggest an adjusted statistic

$$(13) \qquad Q^* = T(T+2) \sum_{k=1}^{m} \frac{\rho^2(k)}{T-k} \quad \sim \quad \chi_K^2.$$

As the sample size increases the terms $(T+2)$ and $(T-k)$ are canceled out. Therefore, the two statistics become equal as the sample size increases towards infinity. The Q*-statistic is the one integrated in the applied statistics package. Moreover, the package provides the probability values associated with the respective Q*-statistic.

The second test is based on a comparison of variances. One property of the random walk hypotheses is the required linearity of the variance during a time interval, i.e., the variance of the sum must equal the sum of the variances. This must also be true for RW2 and RW3. However, this linearity property is more difficult to state for RW2 and RW3 as the variance of increments may be time-varying.

A brief example will illustrate the linearity property. In the RW1 case, where continuously compounded returns r_t are IID, a clear relationship must hold for the variance; that is, for instance, the variance of $r_t + r_{t-1}$ must be twice the variance of r_t. Hence, the test considers the ratio of the two variances and checks whether the ratio is statistically indistinguishable from one. Moreover, the variance ratio is linked to the autocorrelation coefficient in the following way

$$\begin{aligned} VR(2) &= \frac{Var\left[r_t(2)\right]}{2 \cdot Var\left[r_t\right]} = \frac{Var\left[r_t + r_{t-1}\right]}{2 \cdot Var\left[r_t\right]} \\ &= \frac{2 \cdot Var\left[r_t\right] + 2 \cdot Cov\left[r_t, r_{t-1}\right]}{2 \cdot Var\left[r_t\right]}. \\ VR(2) &= 1 + \rho(1) \end{aligned} \tag{14}$$

The above formula uses one- and two-period returns for the comparison of the variances. The formula states that the variance ratio statistic equals one plus the first-order autocorrelation coefficient $\rho(1)$. For stationary time series, $VR(2)$ is one under RW1 as the first-order serial-correlation coefficient $\rho(1)$ is zero. The term $VR(2)$ is greater than one in cases with positive serial correlation and lower than one for time-series with negative autocorrelation. The variance ratio statistic is also applicable for comparisons beyond one- and two-period returns. However, this requires the utilisation of higher order serial correlations, as is shown below.

$$VR(q) = \frac{Var\left[r_t(q)\right]}{q \cdot Var\left[r_t\right]} = 1 + 2 \cdot \sum_{k=1}^{q-1} \left(1 - \frac{k}{q}\right) \cdot \rho(k) \tag{15}$$

The q-period variance ratio statistic $VR(q)$ depends on the serial correlations up to order k. $VR(q)$ is a linear combination of the first $k-1$ serial-correlation coefficients where the weights are linearly declining.

The construction of the statistical tests is slightly different for the different versions of the Random Walk Hypothesis. Following the exposition by Campbell, Lo, and

MacKinlay (1997, pp. 48-55), I briefly outline the procedures for RW1 and RW3 below.[11]

The null hypothesis for RW1 is

$$\mathrm{H}_0: \; r_t = \mu + \varepsilon_t, \qquad \varepsilon_t \text{ IID } N(0, \sigma^2).$$

The log price process is denoted by p_t and $r_t = p_t - p_{t-1}$ represents continuously compounded returns. The data consists of $2n+1$ observations of log prices. Consider the estimators for μ and σ^2 in the two-period case:

$$(16) \qquad \hat{\mu} = \frac{1}{2n} \sum_{k=1}^{2n} (p_k - p_{k-1}) = \frac{1}{2n}(p_{2n} - p_0)$$

$$(17) \qquad \hat{\sigma}_a^2 = \frac{1}{2n} \sum_{k=1}^{2n} (p_k - p_{k-1} - \hat{\mu})^2$$

$$(18) \qquad \hat{\sigma}_b^2 = \frac{1}{2n} \sum_{k=1}^{2n} (p_{2k} - p_{2k-2} - 2 \cdot \hat{\mu})^2$$

The two-period variance ratio and its distribution are given by

$$(19) \qquad \hat{VR}(2) = \frac{\hat{\sigma}_b^2}{\hat{\sigma}_a^2}, \qquad \sqrt{2n}(\hat{VR}(2) - 1) \overset{a}{\sim} N(0, 2).$$

By calculating the standardised statistic $\sqrt{2n}(\hat{VR}(2)-1)/\sqrt{2}$, which is asymptotically standard normal the null hypothesis H_0 can be tested. RW1 is rejected at the 5% level if the test statistic lies outside ± 1.96.

The variance ratio statistics can be generalised to multiperiod returns; however, I do not go into details with respect to this generalisation. Instead, I focus on two refinements which can improve the finite sample properties of the statistics.

[11] I refer the interested reader to Campbell, Lo, and MacKinlay (1997) pp. 48-55 for the full exposition.

The first refinement is to apply overlapping q-period returns, which results in a more efficient variance estimator. In contrast to (18), Campbell, Lo, and MacKinlay suggest the following estimator:

$$\hat{\sigma}_c^2(q) = \frac{1}{nq^2}\sum_{k=q}^{nq}(p_k - p_{k-q} - q\cdot\hat{\mu})^2 , \tag{20}$$

where q represents the return periodicity, which was assumed to be 2 in (18).

The second refinement targets the bias in the variance estimators $\hat{\sigma}_a^2$ and $\hat{\sigma}_c^2$. The unbiased estimators are denoted as $\bar{\sigma}_a^2$ and $\bar{\sigma}_c^2$

$$\bar{\sigma}_a^2(q) = \frac{1}{nq-1}\sum_{k=q}^{nq}(p_k - p_{k-1} - \hat{\mu})^2 \tag{21}$$

$$\bar{\sigma}_c^2(q) = \frac{1}{m}\sum_{k=q}^{nq}(p_k - p_{k-q} - q\cdot\hat{\mu})^2 \tag{22}$$

with

$$m = q\cdot(nq - q + 1)\cdot\left(1 - \frac{q}{nq}\right). \tag{23}$$

This yields the following corrected variance ratio:

$$\overline{VR}(q) = \frac{\bar{\sigma}_c^2(q)}{\bar{\sigma}_a^2} . \tag{24}$$

$\overline{VR}(q)$ is still biased. However, Lo and MacKinlay (1989) report superior performance of this statistic in finite samples compared to $\hat{VR}(q)$. The standardised variance ratio statistic is given by

(25) $$\psi(q) = \sqrt{nq}(\overline{VR}(q) - 1)\left(\frac{2\cdot(2q-1)(q-1)}{3q}\right)^{-1/2} \overset{a}{\sim} N(0,1).$$

The next step is to account for time-varying volatilities. More precisely, a procedure which tests for uncorrelated returns but allows for heteroskedasticity is needed. The above-presented variance ratio test can be modified in such a way. I follow the exposition by Campbell, Lo, and MacKinlay (1997, pp. 54-55), which is based on the work of Lo and MacKinlay (1988), and briefly outline the improved test.

Let $r_t = \mu + \varepsilon_t$ and define the compound null hypothesis H_0^* as shown below:

(H1) For all t, $E(\varepsilon_t) = 0$, and $E(\varepsilon_t \varepsilon_{t-\tau}) = 0$ for any $\tau \neq 0$.

(H2) $\{\varepsilon_t\}$ is ϕ–mixing with coefficients $\phi(m)$ of size $r/(2r-1)$ or is α–mixing with coefficients $\alpha(m)$ of size $r/(r-1)$, where $r > 1$, such that for all t and for any $\tau \geq 0$, there exists some $\delta > 0$ for which $E\left[\left|\varepsilon_t \varepsilon_{t-\tau}\right|^{2(r+\delta)}\right] < \Delta < \infty$.

(H3) $\lim\limits_{nq \longrightarrow \infty} \dfrac{1}{nq} \sum\limits_{t=1}^{nq} E\left[\varepsilon_t^2\right] = \sigma^2 < \infty$.

(H4) For all t, $E\left[\varepsilon_t \varepsilon_{t-j} \varepsilon_t \varepsilon_{t-k}\right] = 0$ for any nonzero j and k where $j \neq k$.

The first condition (H1) represents the uncorrelated increments property of the random walk. This is the property which will be tested. The two conditions (H2) and (H3) impose restrictions on the maximum degree of dependence and heterogeneity. The fourth condition (H4) implies asymptotically uncorrelated sample autocorrelations of ε_t.

The above-stated compound null hypothesis H_0^* allows for quite general forms of heteroskedasticity, including deterministic variance changes and ARCH processes. This allows for a test of the RW3 model.

Under H_0^* the variance ratio $\overline{VR}(q)$ still approaches one. Hence, the asymptotic variance of $\overline{VR}(q)$ has to be computed. This variance will be denoted by $\vartheta(q)$. First, a right-hand-side term of (15) will be reconsidered:

$$\overline{VR}(q) \overset{a}{=} 1 + 2 \cdot \sum_{k=1}^{q-1} \left(1 - \frac{k}{q}\right) \cdot \hat{\rho}(k) . \tag{26}$$

This equality holds asymptotically under quite general conditions. However, in order to obtain an estimator for $\vartheta(q)$, an estimator of the variance of $\hat{\rho}(k)$ is needed. This estimator will be denoted by $\hat{\delta}_k$. Under the null hypothesis H_0^* Lo and MacKinlay (1988) show that

1. The statistic $\overline{VR}(q) - 1$ converges almost surely to zero for all q as n increases without bound.
2. The following is a heteroskedasticity-consistent estimator of δ_k:

$$\hat{\delta}_k = \frac{nq \cdot \sum_{j=k+1}^{nq} (p_j - p_{j-1} - \hat{\mu})^2 \cdot (p_{j-k} - p_{j-k-1} - \hat{\mu})^2}{\left[\sum_{j=1}^{nq} (p_j - p_{j-1} - \hat{\mu})^2 \right]^2} \tag{27}$$

3. The following is a heteroskedasticity-consistent estimator of $\vartheta(q)$:

$$\hat{\vartheta}(q) = 4 \cdot \sum_{k=1}^{q-1} \left(1 - \frac{k}{q}\right)^2 \cdot \hat{\delta}_k \tag{28}$$

The standardised test statistic $\psi^*(q)$ is then given by

$$\psi^*(q) = \frac{\sqrt{nq}(\overline{VR}(q) - 1)}{\sqrt{\hat{\vartheta}}} \overset{a}{\sim} N(0,1) \tag{29}$$

and H_0^* can be tested in the usual way.

Serial correlation might change over time, i.e., there may be times with high autocorrelation and times with low or almost zero serial dependence. In order to obtain a picture of the behaviour of serial correlation through time, additional investigations are conducted. An appealing approach is simple OLS regression analysis. As Campbell, Lo, and MacKinlay (1997, p. 66) describe the R-squared measure of a regression of returns on a constant and its first lag is the square of the slope coefficient. Moreover, the slope coefficient is the first-order serial correlation. Thus, an OLS-approach as shown below yields results which may give indications of the economic significance of serial correlation.

(30) $$y_t = \alpha + \phi_1 y_{t-k} + \varepsilon_t$$

In the above equation y_t is the return of a portfolio at t. This return is regressed on a constant α, and its own lagged value k periods before. ε_t is an error term. There is evidence showing significance in particular of the first lag with short horizon returns. Hence, the regression analyses below focus on first-order serial correlation. However, one disadvantage of the regression approach as well as the autocorrelations is that they do not account for heteroskedasticity. This makes a comparison with the heteroskedasticity consistent estimator appealing.

If serial correlation is time-varying, the lead-lag relationships might be time-varying as well. In order to investigate the evolution of lead-lag relationships over time, an OLS-approach is applied as well. The simplest models tested which account for lead-lag relationships can be formulated as shown below.

(31) $$y_t = \alpha + \phi_2 x_{t-k} + \varepsilon_t$$

The return y_t is regressed on another lagged variable instead of its own lag. In this case x_{t-k} is the return of another portfolio at time $t-k$.

5.3. Results

5.3.1. Autocorrelation Coefficients

The present section provides results on serial correlation at various lags and during different subsample periods. The subsequent results are based on the Q*-statistic which is described in the previous chapter. These results are followed by findings from the above-described OLS-approach.

	BH_RF	BM_RF	BL_RF	SH_RF	SM_RF	SL_RF	MKT_RF	BIG_RF	SML_RF	VAL_RF	GRO_RF	SMB	HML
Panel A: Jul1993-Jun2008													
Lag 1	0.30 *	0.17 *	0.12	0.12	0.31 *	0.29 *	0.15 *	0.27 *	0.32 *	0.27 *	0.24 *	0.15 *	-0.12
Lag 2	0.10	-0.01	0.06	0.13	0.21 *	0.19 *	0.07	0.06	0.17	0.06	0.16 *	-0.05	0.01
Lag 3	0.15	-0.01	0.08	-0.02	-0.02	0.09	0.05	0.07	0.01	0.04	0.11	-0.02	0.24 *
Lag 4	0.14	-0.07	-0.05	-0.09	0.00	0.06	-0.03	0.02	-0.01	-0.04	0.04	-0.03	0.02
Lag 5	0.04	0.13	0.12	0.11	-0.01	0.12	0.14	0.13	0.10	0.09	0.17 *	-0.07	0.01
Lag 6	0.03	0.02	-0.01	0.04	-0.01	0.04	0.01	0.03	0.04	-0.01	0.03	0.08	0.04
Panel B: Jul1993-Jun1998													
Lag 1	0.40 *	0.14	-0.09	0.04	0.25 *	0.08	-0.06	0.27 *	0.22	0.28 *	-0.01	0.17	-0.39 *
Lag 2	0.16	0.12	0.14	0.13	0.16	0.01	0.16	0.18	0.13	0.24	0.13	-0.29 *	0.00
Lag 3	0.23	0.13	0.12	-0.02	-0.09	-0.01	0.12	0.21	-0.09	0.11	0.07	-0.05	0.18
Lag 4	0.25 *	0.22	-0.18	-0.16	-0.20	-0.03	-0.14	0.08	-0.16	0.00	-0.08	0.07	0.09
Lag 5	0.11	-0.16	0.04	0.07	-0.13	0.00	0.02	0.07	0.02	0.10	0.07	-0.05	-0.10
Lag 6	0.20	0.01	-0.10	0.02	-0.05	-0.01	-0.09	0.05	-0.03	0.12	-0.05	-0.01	0.08
Panel C: Jul1998-Jun2003													
Lag 1	0.31 *	0.12	0.18	0.11	0.41 *	0.42 *	0.18	0.23	0.45 *	0.29 *	0.35 *	0.16	-0.02
Lag 2	0.06	-0.15	-0.15	-0.08	0.09	0.15	-0.14	-0.10	0.03	-0.06	0.08	-0.03	0.02
Lag 3	0.08	-0.09	-0.09	-0.16	-0.05	0.12	-0.09	-0.06	-0.01	-0.03	0.11	-0.02	0.35 *
Lag 4	0.07	-0.15	-0.12	-0.18	0.05	0.05	-0.14	-0.08	-0.02	-0.11	0.03	-0.06	-0.03
Lag 5	0.01	0.25 *	0.08	0.10	0.11	0.16	0.12	0.14	0.16	0.08	0.17	-0.25	0.11
Lag 6	0.07	0.06	-0.01	0.09	-0.01	0.04	0.02	0.06	0.06	0.11	0.04	-0.02	0.07
Panel D: Jul2003-Jun2008													
Lag 1	0.17	0.22	0.11	0.10	0.08	-0.12	0.18	0.19	0.01	0.16	-0.03	-0.01	0.03
Lag 2	0.03	0.12	0.08	0.28 *	0.28 *	0.20	0.12	0.13	0.25 *	0.16	0.16	0.07	-0.03
Lag 3	0.12	-0.02	0.17	0.06	-0.09	-0.16	0.08	0.09	-0.08	0.15	-0.05	-0.13	0.13
Lag 4	0.09	0.03	-0.01	0.04	-0.01	-0.07	0.09	0.09	-0.02	0.11	-0.04	-0.23	-0.05
Lag 5	0.00	0.10	0.21	0.19	0.02	0.03	0.22	0.15	0.07	0.10	0.15	0.02	0.02
Lag 6	0.06	0.07	0.19	0.05	0.14	0.06	0.20	0.16	0.10	0.05	0.12	0.18	-0.09

Table 10: Autocorrelation coefficients
The above table shows autocorrelation coefficients up to six lags for the six Fama-French Portfolios, MKT, BIG, SMALL, VALUE, GROWTH, SMB, and HML. Note that SMALL is referred to as SML, VALUE is referred to as VAL, and GROWTH is referred to as GRO. Panel A shows the autocorrelation coefficients for the entire sample period. Panels B, C, and D present coefficients for the three subperiods. The analysis is based on monthly returns. The asterisk * indicates significance at the 5% level.

With respect to forecasting, the above table might be particularly interesting as positive autocorrelation can be an indicator of trends and negative autocorrelation can suggest mean-reverting characteristics. Several portfolios show positive autocorrelation over the entire sample period at the first lag but not at lags two or higher. However, over the whole sample period the highest autocorrelation is found for small caps at lag one. Within the small caps, SM and SL have significant autocorrelation coefficients if test statistics are calculated on the basis of the entire sample period.

The picture changes when subperiods are considered. Between 1993 and 1998 the big value stocks show the strongest positive autocorrelation, followed by HML, which shows significant negative autocorrelation. From 1998 until 2003 the highest positive serial correlation at lag one is found for small caps. This strong positive autocorrelation seems to drive the coefficient for the entire sample period. Again, large value stocks indicate significant positive autocorrelation at the first lag. In the last subsample period, which covers the returns from Jul2003 to Jun2008, the serial correlations at the first lag seem to have vanished. In particular, the strong serial correlation of small caps tends to zero. However, while small value stocks exhibit slightly positive autocorrelation, the serial correlation of small growth stocks is negative. Hence, the zero autocorrelation of small caps might be due to averaging over value and growth stocks. First-order serial correlation in the returns of large value stocks and large neutral stocks is considerable in magnitude but insignificant at the 5% level. The higher autocorrelation of BM seems interesting as it could be related to the migration effects reported by Fama and French (2007a; 2007b). Among those portfolios which exhibit significant autocorrelation over the entire sample period, the returns of big value stocks seem to show the highest consistency with respect to first-order serial correlation.

	Jul1993-Jun2008		Jul1993-Jun1998		Jul1998-Jun2003		Jul2003-Jun2008	
	First Order Serial Correlation and Probability Values							
BH_RF	0.30	*0.0%*	0.40	*0.2%*	0.31	*1.5%*	0.17	*18.9%*
BM_RF	0.17	*2.0%*	0.14	*28.1%*	0.12	*34.7%*	0.22	*8.7%*
BL_RF	0.12	*11.7%*	-0.09	*46.9%*	0.18	*16.0%*	0.10	*40.5%*
SH_RF	0.12	*11.8%*	0.04	*76.5%*	0.11	*38.2%*	0.10	*42.2%*
SM_RF	0.31	*0.0%*	0.25	*4.4%*	0.41	*0.1%*	0.07	*55.2%*
SL_RF	0.29	*0.0%*	0.08	*50.4%*	0.42	*0.1%*	-0.12	*34.6%*
SPI_RF	0.15	*3.8%*	-0.03	*80.4%*	0.15	*22.3%*	0.16	*21.7%*
MKT_RF	0.15	*3.9%*	-0.06	*62.9%*	0.18	*15.8%*	0.18	*16.4%*
BIG_RF	0.27	*0.0%*	0.27	*3.1%*	0.23	*7.3%*	0.19	*13.7%*
SMALL_RF	0.32	*0.0%*	0.22	*7.8%*	0.45	*0.0%*	0.01	*91.9%*
VALUE_RF	0.27	*0.0%*	0.28	*2.7%*	0.29	*2.1%*	0.16	*20.9%*
GROWTH_RF	0.24	*0.1%*	-0.01	*95.5%*	0.35	*0.5%*	-0.03	*79.3%*
SMB	0.15	*4.4%*	0.17	*18.8%*	0.16	*19.5%*	-0.01	*94.6%*
HML	-0.12	*11.7%*	-0.39	*0.2%*	-0.02	*87.4%*	0.03	*80.3%*

Table 11: Serial correlation and probability values
Table 11 presents the first-order autocorrelation coefficients and the associated probability values from the Q*-statistic. The values are shown for the entire sample period as well as for the three subsample periods. Probabilities are given as values in percent and shown in italics.

The probability values presented in Table 11 give a clearer picture on the significance of serial correlations. Considering the entire sample period, almost all portfolios indicate significant autocorrelation at the 5% level. However, large growth stocks, small value stocks, and the returns of the long-short portfolio HML do not show significant autocorrelation at the 10% level. Over the period Jul1993 to Jun2008 serial correlation is positive in all portfolios except HML. Moreover, the autocorrelation coefficients are highly different across the various styles. For instance, small value stocks exhibit serial correlation of 0.12, while big value stocks have a coefficient of 0.30.

The subperiods show different characteristics. The first subsample period exhibits a high dispersion of the autocorrelation coefficients and some portfolios show negative serial correlation. However, significance is weaker during the subsample period considered than over the full sample period. This is also due to the design of the test statistic as fewer observations yields weaker statistical power. Thus, the results of the subperiods cannot be directly compared to those of the entire sample period. Nevertheless, only five portfolios show significant autocorrelation at the 5% level during the period Jul1993 to Jun1998. Interestingly, the small cap portfolio, which contains SH, SM, and SL, exhibits significant serial correlation at the 10% level while

SH and SL are clearly insignificant at this level. An opposite effect can be observed in the last subsample period. It seems that diversification among the portfolios can increase or decrease autocorrelation.

The second subperiod, covering the returns from Jul1998 to Jun2003, confirms the results of the first subsample period. Those portfolios which showed significant autocorrelation in the first subsample period tend to do so in the second subperiod. Despite these tendencies, there are changes as well. The most interesting observation may be the high serial correlation of small growth stocks which is significant at the 0.1% level. The second subperiod covers the tech bubble, which might be a reason for this high autocorrelation as many small tech companies show up in the small growth portfolio. In contrast, the large growth stocks show a much weaker serial correlation. I hypothesise that high and highly significant serial correlation in a particular market segment can be an indicator of a price bubble.

The probability values for the third subsample period confirm the results shown in Table 10. Serial correlation is no longer significant at the 5% level. However, large caps exhibit positive autocorrelation which is significant at the 15% level, and the returns of the BM portfolio are serially correlated with significance at the 10% level. Nevertheless, this is in sharp contrast to the two previous periods.

The above findings indicate a time-varying pattern of serial correlation. In the following, this time variation will be analysed in more detail. In order to do so, a standard OLS regression approach is applied, as is described in Section 5.2. As Table 10 indicates, serial correlation is most apparent at lag one. Hence, the following investigations focus on first-order serial correlation. Again, the analyses are performed for the entire sample as well as for the three subsample periods.

y(t)	y(t-1)	Constant	Coefficient	R^2
	Jul1993-Jun2008			
SH_RF	SH_RF(-1)	0.010	0.12	1.3%
SM_RF	SM_RF(-1)	0.006	0.31	9.8%
SL_RF	SL_RF(-1)	0.007	0.29	8.6%
BH_RF	BH_RF(-1)	0.006	0.31	9.4%
BM_RF	BM_RF(-1)	0.003	0.18	3.0%
BL_RF	BL_RF(-1)	0.005	0.12	1.4%
SMB	SMB(-1)	0.003	0.15	2.2%
HML	HML(-1)	0.001	-0.12	1.4%
MKT_RF	MKT_RF(-1)	0.006	0.15	2.3%
SMALL_RF	SMALL_RF(-1)	0.007	0.32	10.0%
BIG_RF	BIG_RF(-1)	0.005	0.27	7.3%
VALUE_RF	VALUE_RF(-1)	0.007	0.28	7.7%
GROWTH_RF	GROWTH_RF(-1)	0.006	0.24	5.7%

Table 12: Regression approach – full sample
The above table shows the results of regression analyses of the following form:

$$y_t = \alpha + \phi y_{t-1} + \varepsilon_t$$

The returns of the portfolios listed under y(t) are regressed on the lagged returns of the same portfolio plus a constant. The lag is one month, which is indicated by (-1). Each regression includes a constant which is denoted by α. The R-squared measure of the regression is given as a value in percent in the column on the right hand side.

The above table highlights the fact that the R-squared measure of a regression of returns on a constant and its first lag is the square of the slope coefficient. Moreover, the slope coefficient of such a regression represents the autocorrelation coefficient. Thus, the squared slope coefficient equals the R-squared measure which gives a sense of the economic significance of the serial correlation. Thus, for instance, an autocorrelation coefficient of 0.30 yields an R-squared measure of 0.09. In other words, 9% of the monthly variation in the respective portfolio is predictable by using the preceding month's portfolio return.

As Table 12 shows, such magnitudes can be observed for several portfolios such as SL or BH. Over the full sample period, the most significant coefficient results for small caps, followed by the coefficient for large value stocks. Moreover, small caps, large caps as well as value stocks and growth stocks show considerable coefficients and R-squared values. However, most of the high serial correlations in the returns of the four basic styles Small, Large, Value, and Growth are driven by one or two of their constituents. For instance, the autocorrelation in the returns of value stocks is 0.28. The value portfolio consists of small value stocks and large value stocks. Small value stocks exhibit an autocorrelation coefficient of 0.12 and large value stocks, one of 0.31. Hence, the autocorrelation of value stocks seems to be strongly influenced by the serial correlation in the returns of large value stocks. Similar observations also hold for the other style portfolios. However, besides styles and combined styles there are the returns of the aggregate market. The coefficient amounts to 0.15, but the R-squared measure is at a fairly low 2.3%. This again points at a possible diversification effect.

y(t)	y(t-1)	Constant	Coefficient	R^2
	Panel A: Jul1993-Jun1998			
SH_RF	SH_RF(-1)	0.013	0.04	0.1%
SM_RF	SM_RF(-1)	0.009	0.26	6.7%
SL_RF	SL_RF(-1)	0.013	0.08	0.7%
BH_RF	BH_RF(-1)	0.009	0.40	16.9%
BM_RF	BM_RF(-1)	0.012	0.14	1.9%
BL_RF	BL_RF(-1)	0.019	-0.09	0.8%
SMB	SMB(-1)	-0.003	0.17	2.8%
HML	HML(-1)	-0.001	-0.39	16.6%
MKT_RF	MKT_RF(-1)	0.018	-0.06	0.4%
SMALL_RF	SMALL_RF(-1)	0.011	0.22	5.0%
BIG_RF	BIG_RF(-1)	0.012	0.27	7.4%
VALUE_RF	VALUE_RF(-1)	0.011	0.28	8.0%
GROWTH_RF	GROWTH_RF(-1)	0.016	-0.01	0.0%
	Panel B: Jul1998-Jun2003			
SH_RF	SH_RF(-1)	0.001	0.11	1.2%
SM_RF	SM_RF(-1)	-0.002	0.41	17.2%
SL_RF	SL_RF(-1)	-0.004	0.42	17.7%
BH_RF	BH_RF(-1)	0.000	0.31	9.5%
BM_RF	BM_RF(-1)	-0.011	0.12	1.4%
BL_RF	BL_RF(-1)	-0.006	0.18	3.3%
SMB	SMB(-1)	0.002	0.16	2.7%
HML	HML(-1)	0.005	0.00	0.0%
MKT_RF	MKT_RF(-1)	-0.006	0.18	3.3%
SMALL_RF	SMALL_RF(-1)	-0.001	0.45	20.3%
BIG_RF	BIG_RF(-1)	-0.005	0.23	5.1%
VALUE_RF	VALUE_RF(-1)	0.000	0.29	8.6%
GROWTH_RF	GROWTH_RF(-1)	-0.004	0.36	12.7%
	Panel C: Jul2003-Jun2008			
SH_RF	SH_RF(-1)	0.017	0.10	1.0%
SM_RF	SM_RF(-1)	0.017	0.07	0.5%
SL_RF	SL_RF(-1)	0.025	-0.10	1.0%
BH_RF	BH_RF(-1)	0.008	0.20	3.5%
BM_RF	BM_RF(-1)	0.006	0.26	6.0%
BL_RF	BL_RF(-1)	0.007	0.13	1.6%
SMB	SMB(-1)	0.010	0.00	0.0%
HML	HML(-1)	0.000	0.02	0.0%
MKT_RF	MKT_RF(-1)	0.006	0.22	4.3%
SMALL_RF	SMALL_RF(-1)	0.020	0.02	0.0%
BIG_RF	BIG_RF(-1)	0.007	0.23	4.8%
VALUE_RF	VALUE_RF(-1)	0.012	0.18	2.9%
GROWTH_RF	GROWTH_RF(-1)	0.016	-0.01	0.0%

Table 13: Regression approach – subsamples
The above table shows the results of regression analyses of the following form:

$$y_t = \alpha + \phi y_{t-1} + \varepsilon_t$$

The returns of the portfolios listed under y(t) are regressed on the lagged returns of the same portfolio plus a constant. The lag is one month, which is indicated by (-1). Each regression includes a constant which is denoted by α. The R-squared measure of the regression is given as a value in percent in the column on the right hand side. The three panels refer to the three subsample periods.

As expected, the coefficients of Table 13 are consistent with those of Tables 10 and 11. However, the R-squared measure might be a more intuitive value than the probabilities provided before. Consistent with the previous findings, there are quite strong autocorrelations for the full sample period. Moreover, serial correlation is even stronger for some of the portfolios during the first two subsample periods with R-squared measures up to 20%. In contrast, the autocorrelation coefficients, and thus R-squared measures, drop in the last subperiod, which covers the data from Jul2003 to Jun2008.

To my knowledge there is no investigation of the Random Walk Hypothesis for combined style portfolios based on data of the Swiss stock market. Thus, comparisons of the results are difficult and have to be interpreted with caution. However, as outlined in the literature review section, there is research on serial correlation with respect to size-sorted portfolios which may be compared to the above findings.

The above evidence on positive autocorrelation is consistent with the early findings of Fisher (1966), who finds positive autocorrelation in monthly returns of diversified portfolios. Lo and MacKinlay (1988), Conrad and Kaul (1988), McInish and Wood (1991) as well as Mech (1993) find small cap portfolios to show stronger positive autocorrelation than large cap portfolios. As can be seen from Table 12, this agrees with my findings for the full sample period. In contrast, autocorrelation is stronger in the large cap portfolio in two of the three subperiods. Although Lewellen (2002) investigates size and book-to-market sorted portfolios, his results cannot be compared as he uses 12-month returns and focuses on momentum issues.

So far, the investigations have concentrated on the full sample period and three subsample periods of equal length. However, the subsample periods are chosen arbitrarily; hence, a certain subperiod might show especially significant or especially insignificant results. Moreover, three subperiods might have limited informative value with respect to the evolution of serial correlation across time. In the following I address this issue.

In order to obtain a more comprehensive picture of time-varying aspects, I run the same regression analyses as above for various time periods. The periods are all of the same length and cover data of 60 months. For instance, the first regression uses the returns from Jul1993 to Jun1998. The second regression uses the data from Aug1993 to Jul1998 and so on. I run regressions for each of the above-mentioned portfolios and for each 60-month window. The result is a time series of regression outputs such as the constant, the coefficients, and the R-squared measures. The approach enables the plotting of outputs over time.

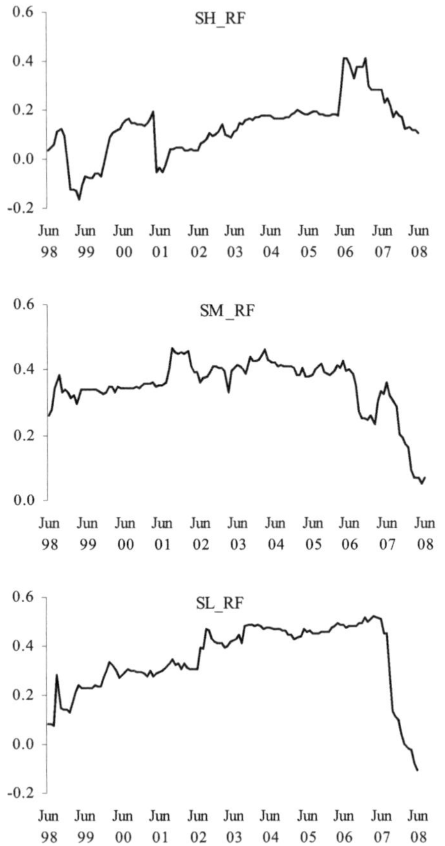

Figure 2: Coefficients of rolling fixed windows – small cap portfolios
The above figure shows the coefficients ϕ of a regression analysis with progressing fixed windows. The regression is of the form:

$$y_t = \alpha + \phi y_{t-1} + \varepsilon_t$$

The returns of the portfolios listed at the top of each chart are regressed on the lagged returns of the same portfolio plus a constant which is denoted by α. The Y-axis refers to the magnitude of the coefficient. The X-axis refers to the date of the last observation of a 60-month window.

Figure 2 tracks the coefficients of the three portfolios SH, SM, and SL for each of the 60-month estimation period. The analyses reveal new facts on the economic significance of the serial correlation across time. For instance, the analyses based on the three subsample periods indicate a declining autocorrelation during Jul2003 to Jun2008. The above figure sheds new light on this evolution. All three small cap portfolios show quite strong serial correlation up to mid-2007. SH and SL even show increasing autocorrelation until 2007. This can be interpreted as evidence of trend building in small value and small growth stocks. Moreover, the vanishing serial correlation shown in the previous analyses seems almost entirely attributable to the last year of the sample period. In other words, if the last subsample period were Jul2002 to Jun2007 instead of Jul2003 to Jun2008, the autocorrelation coefficients would suggest high serial correlation. However, the plots may be somewhat misleading. For example, the last data point in 2008 is calculated with data ranging from Jul2003 until Jun2008. Hence, autocorrelation might have decreased earlier than it appears in the charts.

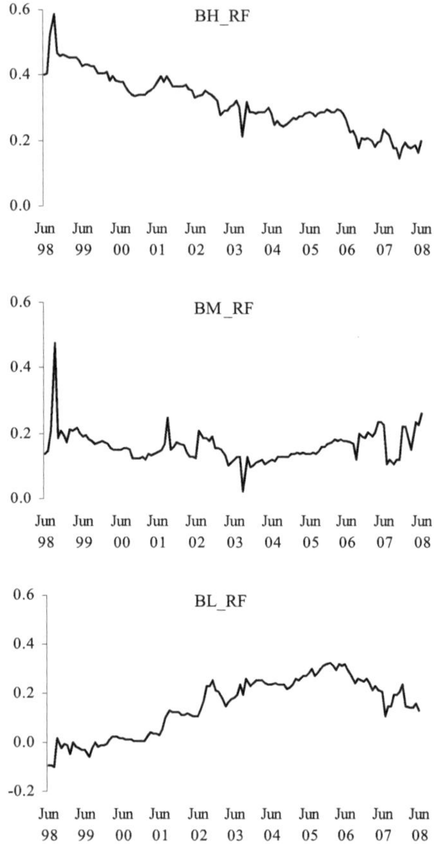

Figure 3: Coefficients of rolling fixed windows – large cap portfolios
The above figure shows the coefficients ϕ of a regression analysis with progressing fixed windows. The regression is of the form:

$$y_t = \alpha + \phi y_{t-1} + \varepsilon_t$$

The returns of the portfolios listed at the top of each chart are regressed on the lagged returns of the same portfolio plus a constant which is denoted by α. The Y-axis refers to the magnitude of the coefficient. The X-axis refers to the date of the last observation of a 60-month window.

Figure 3 exhibits the time-series of the coefficients of the large cap portfolios. The plots contrast with those of the small cap portfolios. The returns of large value stocks show declining serial correlation throughout the entire sample period. However, the autocorrelation coefficient levels out at around 0.2, which yields an R-squared measure of approximately 4%. The serial correlation of the large growth stocks increased over time but decreased toward the end of the sample period. The returns of large caps which are not allocated to growth or value do not show a clear picture of serial correlation as the time-series shows several spikes. A possible reason might be high turnovers compared to the other portfolios. Recall that the portfolios are constructed each year according to a double ranking based on size and price-to-book ratios. Thus, on the one hand, changing price-to-book ratios cause some value stocks to migrate to the neutral portfolios. On the other hand, changing price-to-book ratios also cause some growth stocks to migrate to the neutral portfolios. In contrast, jumps from value to growth or vice versa are much less likely.[12]

[12] Fama and French (2007a; 2007b) investigate the effects of migration on returns in detail.

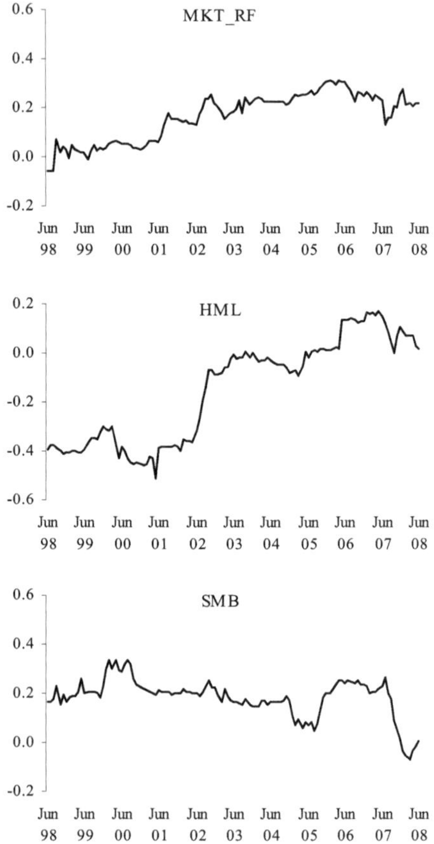

Figure 4: Coefficients of rolling fixed windows – market and long-short portfolios
The above figure shows the coefficients ϕ of a regression analysis with progressing fixed windows. The regression is of the form:

$$y_t = \alpha + \phi y_{t-1} + \varepsilon_t$$

The returns of the portfolios listed at the top of each chart are regressed on the lagged returns of the same portfolio plus a constant which is denoted by α. The Y-axis refers to the magnitude of the coefficient. The X-axis refers to the date of the last observation of a 60-month window.

Figure 4 plots the time-series of the coefficients of the aggregate market returns and the returns of the two long-short portfolios SMB and HML. The coefficients for MKT are quite similar to those of the BL portfolio. The reason is the value weighted returns. The Swiss stock market is dominated by a few stocks which account for the majority of the market capitalisation. During the sample period, these stocks can often be allocated to the BL portfolio; hence, the returns of the BL portfolio are close to those of the aggregate market. The coefficients of HML show an interesting pattern. At the beginning in 1998 the serial correlation is considerably negative, which indicates mean reversion characteristics of this portfolio. In other words, a month's negative return of HML tends to be followed by a positive return and vice versa. However, as time passes, the negative autocorrelation disappears and turns into slight positive serial correlation. However, its magnitude and R-squared measure is fairly low. The returns of SMB exhibit low positive autocorrelation during the sample period. Nevertheless, serial correlation of SMB returns is far from constant through time.

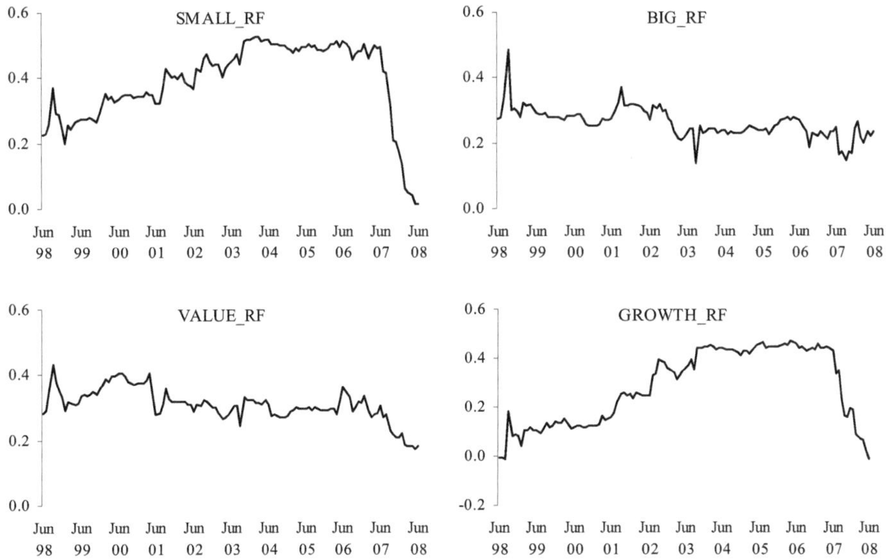

Figure 5: Coefficients of rolling fixed windows – four style portfolios
The above figure shows the coefficients ϕ of a regression analysis with progressing fixed windows. The regression is of the form:

$$y_t = \alpha + \phi y_{t-1} + \varepsilon_t$$

The returns of the portfolios listed at the top of each chart are regressed on the lagged returns of the same portfolio plus a constant which is denoted by α . The Y-axis refers to the magnitude of the coefficient. The X-axis refers to the date of the last observation of a 60-month window.

Figure 5 plots the time series of the regression outputs for the four remaining style portfolios. All four styles exhibit some serial correlation during certain time periods.

The autocorrelation of small caps follows the pattern of the small growth stocks, which is discussed above. However, autocorrelation in small cap returns seems strong until mid-2007, when serial correlation sharply drops. In contrast, large caps do not show such strong serial correlation. The pattern is similar to that of the returns of BM stocks. Value stocks exhibit serial correlation between 0.2 and 0.4 throughout a majority of the sample period. The returns of growth stocks show weak autocorrelation at the first estimation windows. However, serial correlation in the growth portfolio increased over time. The four style portfolios share two common characteristics with respect to serial correlation. First, serial correlation has weakened during the most recent estimation windows. Second, there is no negative autocorrelation in the returns of the four basic style portfolios. This is in contrast to the returns of the combined style portfolios. Again, diversification across size or valuation affects the patterns of serial correlation.

The findings presented in this section provide considerable evidence of serial correlation in some of the investigated portfolios. Moreover, autocorrelation seems to change over time and might be significant during some time intervals and insignificant during others. I conclude that the above evidence suggests a rejection of the RW1 model. However, as outlined in Chapter 3, the RW1 model is quite restrictive and does not allow for heteroskedasticity. Hence, a heteroskedasticitiy-consistent test is applied in the following section.

5.3.2. Variance Ratios

This section provides the results of tests on the RW3 model which accounts for time-varying volatility patterns. The applied test procedure is described in detail in section 5.2. However, the basic idea of the test can be captured by the following formula:

$$\overline{VR}(q) = \frac{\overline{\sigma}_c^2(q)}{\overline{\sigma}_a^2} \tag{32}$$

The variance of multi-period returns $\bar{\sigma}_c^2(q)$ is set in relation to the variance of single-period returns $\bar{\sigma}_a^2$. If the Random Walk Hypothesis holds, the variance is a linear function of the time interval. However, in order to account for time-varying variances a particular test statistic is required which is given as

$$(33) \qquad \psi^*(q) = \frac{\sqrt{nq}(\overline{VR}(q)-1)}{\sqrt{\hat{\vartheta}}} \overset{a}{\sim} N(0,1).$$

Thus, the RW3 model can be rejected at the 5% level if the test statistic $\psi^*(q)$ exceeds ± 1.96. In the following, this test is conducted for the portfolios analysed above. I focus on first-order serial correlation and the results obtained by using $q = 2$.[13]

Portfolio	VR(2)	Psi(2)	Psi*(2)
	Jul1993-Jun2008		
SH_RF	1.12	1.66	1.41
SM_RF	1.32	4.33	3.49
SL_RF	1.30	4.09	2.61
BH_RF	1.29	3.90	3.24
BM_RF	1.18	2.36	1.44
BL_RF	1.12	1.65	1.41
SMB	1.16	2.09	1.98
HML	0.88	-1.64	-1.43
MKT_RF	1.15	2.05	1.72
SPI_RF	1.15	2.05	1.72
SMALL_RF	1.33	4.38	3.40
BIG_RF	1.27	3.59	2.42
VALUE_RF	1.27	3.62	3.29
GROWTH_RF	1.25	3.32	2.48

Table 14: Variance ratios and test statistics (q=2) – full sample
The above table shows the variance ratios and two test statistics for the six Fama-French Portfolios, SMALL, BIG, VALUE, GROWTH, MKT, and the Swiss Performance Index. The variance ratios are shown in the column marked VR(2). The biased test statistic is shown in the column denoted Psi(2). The corrected test statistic which accounts for heteroskedasticity is presented in the column marked Psi*(2). The variance ratios are calculated by using two-period returns which is indicated by (2).

Table 14 presents the variance ratios of the portfolio returns and its associated test statistics. In order to provide some intuition on the results, I repeat equation (26) from section 5.2.:

[13] Generally the variance ratios increase if $q = 4$ is used which implies serial correlation in multiperiod returns. The results from applying $q = 4$ are presented in the appendix.

(34) $$\overline{VR}(q) \overset{a}{=} 1 + 2 \cdot \sum_{k=1}^{q-1} \left(1 - \frac{k}{q}\right) \cdot \hat{\rho}(k)$$

In the case of two-period returns and first-order serial correlation, the formula simplifies to

(35) $$\overline{VR}(2) \overset{a}{=} 1 + \hat{\rho}(1) .$$

Hence, the variance ratio equals approximately one plus the first-order serial correlation of the respective portfolio returns. The findings of section 5.3.1. suggest variance ratios greater than one for the majority of the portfolios. Comparing the values of Table 14 to those of Tables 10 and 12 confirms this relationship. Except for HML, there is positive serial correlation in the returns of the portfolios investigated.

However, Table 14 reveals additional insights of serial correlation with respect to significance. The column Psi(2) provides statistics which have the power to test the RW1 model but not the RW3 model. The column marked Psi*(2) provides the values of the corrected test statistic which accounts for heteroskedasticity. As we can see, the values of the corrected test are less significant than those of the biased test. Nevertheless, various portfolios show significant serial correlation at the 5% level. This indicates a rejection of the RW3 model for certain market segments.

Fairly strong positive first-order serial correlation can be observed in the returns of small neutral stocks, big value stocks, small caps, and value stocks in general. Further significant autocorrelation at the 5% level can also be found in the returns of small growth stocks, SMB, large caps, and general growth stocks. In contrast, there are some portfolios where the significance disappears as it is accounted for heteroskedasticity. This is true for the market proxy MKT, the SPI, and the returns of the big neutral stocks. In other words, a test which does not account for heteroskedasticity suggests the rejection of the random walk model for aggregate market returns. In contrast, an improved test is not able to reject the random walk model for the returns of the aggregate market. This seems interesting and might highlight the superiority of the variance ratio test compared to the Q-statistics. However, there are also portfolios which do not show serial correlation in both tests. The portfolio returns of small value stocks, large growth stocks, and HML do not exhibit significant serial correlation at all. The only portfolio with significant negative autocorrelation is HML.

Portfolio	Jul1993-Jun1998			Jul1998-Jun2003			Jul2003-Jun2008		
	VR(2)	Psi(2)	Psi*(2)	VR(2)	Psi(2)	Psi*(2)	VR(2)	Psi(2)	Psi*(2)
SH_RF	1.07	0.51	0.40	1.15	1.14	1.13	1.11	0.81	1.00
SM_RF	1.28	2.17	1.78	1.46	3.56	3.02	1.09	0.70	0.87
SL_RF	1.12	0.93	1.03	1.46	3.57	2.92	0.88	-0.93	-0.97
BH_RF	1.42	3.25	3.28	1.35	2.71	2.25	1.12	0.96	1.10
BM_RF	1.17	1.31	1.26	1.16	1.20	0.90	1.16	1.26	1.46
BL_RF	0.93	-0.54	-0.48	1.20	1.58	1.54	1.11	0.87	0.89
SMB	1.20	1.58	1.35	1.20	1.57	1.64	1.00	0.04	0.03
HML	0.59	-3.21	-2.90	0.99	-0.05	-0.04	1.05	0.37	0.43
MKT_RF	0.96	-0.30	-0.26	1.21	1.61	1.50	1.14	1.10	1.29
SPI_RF	1.00	0.01	0.01	1.18	1.41	1.00	1.12	0.94	1.09
SMALL_RF	1.26	2.00	1.71	1.50	3.85	3.36	1.01	0.11	0.14
BIG_RF	1.31	2.41	2.26	1.26	2.05	1.54	1.14	1.06	1.33
VALUE_RF	1.31	2.39	2.55	1.33	2.57	2.38	1.13	0.98	1.24
GROWTH_RF	1.02	0.17	0.15	1.39	3.01	2.70	0.96	-0.31	-0.49

Table 15: Variance ratios and test statistics (q=2) – subsamples
The above table shows the variance ratios and two test statistics for the six Fama-French Portfolios, SMALL, BIG, VALUE, GROWTH, MKT, and the Swiss Performance Index. The variance ratios are shown in the column marked VR(2). The biased test statistic is shown in the column denoted Psi(2). The corrected test statistic which accounts for heteroskedasticity is presented in the column marked Psi*(2). The variance ratios are calculated by using two-period returns, which is indicated by (2).

The results of the variance ratio test for the three subsample periods are shown in Table 15. However, the number of observations in the subsamples is restricted to 60 monthly returns. Moreover, the corrections described in section 5.2. lead to deviations between the serial correlations of Table 15, which can be derived from the variance ratios, and those of Tables 10 and 13, which have been estimated by a regression approach.

Despite the corrections, the autocorrelation coefficients tend to be of about the same magnitude as in the previous analyses. However, accounting for heteroskedasticity causes some previously significant autocorrelations to become insignificant. For instance, in the first subsample period this is the case for the returns of the small neutral portfolio and for the overall small cap portfolio.

On the basis of weekly returns from September 6, 1962 to December 26, 1985, Lo and MacKinlay (1988) reject the Random Walk Hypothesis for a variety of portfolios. With respect to a broad index of AMEX and NYSE stocks the rejection of the random walk model is stronger for equal weighted returns than for value-weighted returns and stronger in the first half of the sample period than in the second half. Campbell, Lo, and MacKinlay (1997, p. 69) attribute this finding to an increasing competitiveness of financial markets over time. This interpretation might also apply to the above evidence, which shows vanishing serial correlation during the last subsample period. Moreover, Lo and MacKinlay (1988) investigate the returns of size sorted portfolios. On the basis of weekly returns they reject the RW3 model for all portfolios.[14] However, by using four-week returns the Random Walk Hypothesis cannot be rejected for the portfolios consisting of the largest stocks. In contrast, the null hypothesis can still be rejected for the returns of small cap portfolios. This seems to support the evidence presented in this section as the RW3 model can be rejected for the two small cap portfolios SM and SL as well as for the large cap portfolio BH.

Summing up, the evidence of the above variance ratio tests suggests a rejection of the RW3 model for certain market segments. Over the entire sample period the tests reject the RW3 model at the 5% level for SM, SL, BH, SMB, and all four basic style portfolios. In contrast, the RW3 hypothesis cannot be rejected for the aggregate market portfolio. However, the results of the subsample periods are mixed. On the one hand, the RW3 model can be rejected in the first two subsample periods for various portfolios. On the other hand, the RW3 model cannot be rejected at the 5% level for any portfolio in the third subperiod.

[14] Similar findings for the RW3 model can be found, for instance, in Boudoukh, Richardson, and Whitelaw (1994) or for the RW1 model in Hameed (1997).

5.4. Summary of Empirical Part I

In Chapter 5 two procedures are applied in order to test the random walk model. One test is based on the coefficients of serial correlation. The other test considers variance ratios and accounts for possible heteroskedasticity.

On the basis of monthly data ranging from Jul1993 to Jun2008, serial correlation appears in the returns of various portfolios. Among the six Fama-French Portfolios significant serial correlation can be found in large value stocks, large neutral stocks, small neutral stocks, and small growth stocks. Over the entire sample period all style based portfolios as well as the market indices SPI and MKT exhibit significant first order serial correlation. The autocorrelation is positive in all of the previously mentioned portfolios. The strongest autocorrelation is found in the returns of small caps. This is supported by the findings of Lo and MacKinlay (1988), Mech (1993), and others. However, small value stocks do not exhibit significant autocorrelation in any of the investigated time periods. Of the two long-short portfolios only SMB shows significant autocorrelation over the full sample period. The only case with significant negative serial correlation appears in the returns of HML during the first subsample period. Serial correlation seems to be less significant in each of the subperiods. In the last subperiod none of the portfolios shows significant first-order serial correlation. However, regression analyses revealed more insight on the evolution of autocorrelations over time. In particular, small caps exhibit considerable coefficient values until mid-2007.

The variance ratio tests confirm some of the findings of the autocorrelation analyses. First-order serial correlation seems to be nothing unusual over the entire sample period and in the first two subsample periods, which cover the time period Jul1993 to Jun2003. However, accounting for heteroskedasticity clearly lowers the significance of the serial correlation. Moreover, serial correlation in aggregate market returns disappears. This reveals a certain influence of time-varying volatility and points out the possibility of uncorrelated aggregate market returns but serially correlated returns of some (combined) style portfolios.

The above evidence suggests a rejection of the null hypothesis that the returns of the Fama-French Portfolios follow a random walk. Moreover, serial correlation seems to change over time. Returns of a certain portfolio might be serially uncorrelated in one period but show autocorrelation during another period. However, the positive serial correlation in the returns of large value stocks seems to be the most consistent. However, the vanishing autocorrelation during the last sample period raises the question of whether serial correlation in the returns of certain (combined) style portfolios has been exploited by market participants or whether it is a particularity of the most recent time period.

6. Forecasting Models

6.1. Implied and Estimated Cross-Autocorrelation

As outlined in the literature review section, Lo and MacKinlay (1990a) identify a lead-lag relationship between the returns of small cap portfolios and the returns of large cap portfolios. The relationship is documented for return periods of up to four weeks. Thus, it seems an appealing approach to apply this finding in a forecasting model. In contrast, Bodoukh, Richardson, and Whitelaw (1994) argue that, even in a world in which large-firm returns are not more informative than the returns of small caps, there can be considerable cross-serial correlation. However, it cannot be ruled out that we live in a world where the returns of large caps (or other market segments) carry important information with respect to forecasting.

Therefore, as a starting point, I investigate the argument by Boudoukh, Richardson, and Whitelaw (1994) that estimated cross-serial correlations can be approximated by the product of contemporaneous correlations and serial correlations. The results might be important for the subsequent model-building process. For instance, large differences between estimated cross-serial correlation and implied cross-serial correlation could suggest some information which might be exploited in a forecasting model.

I start this analysis by estimating the cross-serial correlations of the six Fama-French Portfolios, MKT, the four basic style portfolios SMALL, BIG, VALUE, GROWTH, and the two long-short portfolios SMB and HML. As before, the investigations are based on monthly returns of the time period Jul1993 to Jun2008. Moreover, the full sample period is divided into three subsample periods of 60 months' length each, which are also investigated.

	BH_RF	BM_RF	BL_RF	SH_RF	SM_RF	SL_RF	MKT_RF	BIG_RF	SML_RF	VAL_RF	GRO_RF	SMB	HML
BH_RF(-1)	0.31	0.20	0.22	0.28	0.33	0.36	0.22	0.27	0.38	0.34	0.35	0.16	-0.08
BM_RF(-1)	0.25	0.17	0.10	0.30	0.29	0.33	0.12	0.20	0.35	0.31	0.27	0.23	0.01
BL_RF(-1)	0.26	0.24	0.12	0.25	0.27	0.25	0.14	0.24	0.29	0.29	0.22	0.07	0.06
SH_RF(-1)	0.09	0.08	-0.02	0.12	0.26	0.21	0.00	0.07	0.22	0.12	0.13	0.24	-0.05
SM_RF(-1)	0.19	0.15	0.06	0.27	0.31	0.28	0.07	0.16	0.33	0.26	0.22	0.26	0.02
SL_RF(-1)	0.18	0.09	0.02	0.20	0.24	0.29	0.03	0.12	0.28	0.22	0.21	0.25	-0.02
MKT_RF(-1)	0.27	0.24	0.13	0.28	0.29	0.28	0.15	0.25	0.32	0.32	0.25	0.10	0.04
BIG_RF(-1)	0.31	0.23	0.17	0.32	0.34	0.37	0.18	0.27	0.39	0.36	0.32	0.19	-0.01
SMALL_RF(-1)	0.18	0.12	0.02	0.22	0.30	0.30	0.04	0.13	0.32	0.23	0.21	0.29	-0.02
VALUE_RF(-1)	0.24	0.17	0.13	0.24	0.35	0.34	0.14	0.21	0.36	0.28	0.29	0.23	-0.08
GROWTH_RF(-1)	0.24	0.17	0.07	0.25	0.29	0.31	0.09	0.19	0.32	0.28	0.24	0.20	0.01
SMB(-1)	-0.20	-0.16	-0.22	-0.15	-0.07	-0.10	-0.22	-0.22	-0.12	-0.21	-0.17	0.15	-0.02
HML(-1)	-0.04	-0.04	0.07	-0.06	0.02	-0.02	0.05	-0.01	-0.02	-0.06	0.02	0.00	-0.12

Table 16: Cross-autocorrelation coefficients – Jul1993-Jun2008

Table 16 shows the cross-autocorrelation coefficients of the portfolios under investigation. The (-1) indicates a lag of one in the calculations. The calculations are based on monthly returns. In the top line, SMALL, VALUE, and GROWTH are abbreviated and referred to as SML, VAL, and GRO, respectively.

The table above confirms the findings of Lo and MacKinlay (1990a) for the Swiss stock market. Focusing on the two portfolios BIG and SMALL, we can see that the cross-autocorrelation between BIG_RF(-1) and SMALL_RF is 0.39. In contrast, the cross-autocorrelation for SMALL_RF(-1) and BIG_RF is 0.13. This asymmetrical relationship suggests a lead-lag relationship between these two portfolios, with large caps leading small caps.

The formation of the six Fama-French Portfolios allows additional analyses. For example, it might be interesting to have a look at the intersectional portfolios with the strongest cross-autocorrelation. Before doing so, some earlier findings from the descriptive statistics section are repeated. The partition in value and growth stocks was done with respect to the market-to-book ratio. Intuitively, this might lead to the conclusion that small growth stocks are on average larger than small value stocks. The calculation of the average market capitalisation in Table 3 supports this intuition somewhat. However, a breakdown according to size only might hide the impact of valuation ratios.

Turning to the intersectional portfolios, I consider various leaders for the same lagged variable. The first lagged variable under consideration is SMALL_RF (SML_RF), which seems to be lead by BIG_RF, with a cross-autocorrelation coefficient of 0.39. The question is now which of the large cap portfolios shows the highest cross-autocorrelation with SMALL_RF. The answer is BH_RF(-1), followed by BM_RF(-1), and BL_RF(-1). With respect to forecasting this could suggest a model with big value stocks as predictors. Another question is which of the small cap portfolios has the highest cross-autocorrelation with BIG_RF(-1). The answer is SL_RF. In other words, large caps seem to be strongly cross-autocorrelated with small growth stocks and the large caps seem to lead the small growth stocks. A next step is to analyse which of the large cap portfolios has the strongest cross-autocorrelation with the small growth stocks, and the answer is large value stocks.

An analysis of the two long-short portfolios SMB and HML over the entire sample period leaves little hope of any forecasting power. Both portfolios show low positive or low negative cross-autocorrelations with every other portfolio under consideration.

For forecasting purposes it is important to have knowledge about the robustness of the relationships over time. Therefore, the cross-autocorrelation coefficients for the subperiods are provided below.

	BH_RF	BM_RF	BL_RF	SH_RF	SM_RF	SL_RF	MKT_RF	BIG_RF	SML_RF	VAL_RF	GRO_RF	SMB	HML
BH_RF(-1)	0.41	0.32	0.25	0.33	0.49	0.45	0.28	0.40	0.49	0.44	0.40	0.14	0.00
BM_RF(-1)	0.28	0.15	0.05	0.21	0.22	0.05	0.07	0.19	0.18	0.29	0.06	0.00	0.26
BL_RF(-1)	0.31	0.06	-0.09	0.06	0.16	-0.03	-0.07	0.11	0.07	0.22	-0.07	-0.05	0.34
SH_RF(-1)	0.03	0.11	-0.02	0.04	0.24	0.12	-0.01	0.04	0.16	0.04	0.05	0.16	-0.03
SM_RF(-1)	0.19	0.16	-0.08	0.21	0.27	0.18	-0.05	0.11	0.26	0.24	0.06	0.22	0.20
SL_RF(-1)	0.22	0.18	0.02	0.13	0.25	0.08	0.04	0.17	0.18	0.21	0.06	0.02	0.16
MKT_RF(-1)	0.31	0.07	-0.08	0.07	0.17	-0.03	-0.06	0.12	0.08	0.23	-0.06	-0.05	0.35
BIG_RF(-1)	0.40	0.21	0.08	0.24	0.35	0.18	0.11	0.28	0.30	0.38	0.15	0.03	0.25
SMALL_RF(-1)	0.16	0.17	-0.03	0.15	0.30	0.15	-0.01	0.12	0.23	0.19	0.07	0.15	0.12
VALUE_RF(-1)	0.26	0.26	0.14	0.22	0.44	0.34	0.16	0.26	0.39	0.29	0.27	0.18	-0.02
GROWTH_RF(-1)	0.29	0.13	-0.04	0.11	0.23	0.03	-0.02	0.15	0.14	0.24	-0.01	-0.02	0.28
SMB(-1)	-0.33	-0.06	-0.15	-0.12	-0.08	-0.05	-0.15	-0.22	-0.10	-0.27	-0.11	0.16	-0.17
HML(-1)	-0.07	0.13	0.21	0.13	0.23	0.37	0.21	0.11	0.28	0.04	0.32	0.24	-0.39

Table 17: Cross-autocorrelation coefficients – Jul1993-Jun1998
Table 17 shows the cross-autocorrelation coefficients of the portfolios under investigation. The (-1) indicates a lag of one in the calculations. The calculations are based on monthly returns. In the top line, SMALL, VALUE, and GROWTH are abbreviated and referred to as SML, VAL, and GRO, respectively.

Table 17 represents the cross-autocorrelations for the first subsample period. Two findings seem worthy of mention. First, there are more extreme cross-autocorrelation coefficients in the subperiod considered than over the full sample period. This is especially striking for the relationships between large value stocks and small caps. The leading role of large value stocks is more pronounced for the period of Jul1993 until Jun1998 than for the entire sample period. In addition, the lead-lag relationship might be weaker for small value stocks than for small growth stocks and small medium stocks. Second, the large growth stocks show almost no cross-autocorrelation with the two small cap portfolios SH and SL. Overall, Table 17 mostly confirms the results found for the full sample period.

	BH_RF	BM_RF	BL_RF	SH_RF	SM_RF	SL_RF	MKT_RF	BIG_RF	SML_RF	VAL_RF	GRO_RF	SMB	HML
BH_RF(-1)	0.31	0.12	0.14	0.23	0.28	0.38	0.13	0.20	0.36	0.32	0.33	0.23	-0.13
BM_RF(-1)	0.29	0.13	0.03	0.32	0.29	0.39	0.05	0.17	0.40	0.35	0.30	0.35	-0.05
BL_RF(-1)	0.34	0.31	0.19	0.40	0.34	0.38	0.22	0.32	0.43	0.42	0.35	0.14	-0.06
SH_RF(-1)	0.17	0.08	-0.08	0.12	0.27	0.29	-0.04	0.08	0.28	0.17	0.18	0.31	-0.09
SM_RF(-1)	0.33	0.18	0.11	0.36	0.41	0.41	0.12	0.23	0.45	0.39	0.34	0.33	-0.06
SL_RF(-1)	0.29	0.08	0.01	0.28	0.32	0.43	0.02	0.14	0.42	0.34	0.31	0.41	-0.09
MKT_RF(-1)	0.34	0.28	0.17	0.39	0.34	0.41	0.19	0.29	0.44	0.42	0.36	0.20	-0.07
BIG_RF(-1)	0.34	0.19	0.11	0.34	0.33	0.43	0.13	0.24	0.43	0.39	0.35	0.28	-0.09
SMALL_RF(-1)	0.32	0.12	0.02	0.31	0.39	0.45	0.04	0.17	0.45	0.36	0.33	0.42	-0.09
VALUE_RF(-1)	0.29	0.12	0.05	0.21	0.32	0.40	0.06	0.17	0.38	0.30	0.31	0.31	-0.13
GROWTH_RF(-1)	0.35	0.18	0.08	0.36	0.37	0.46	0.11	0.23	0.47	0.41	0.37	0.35	-0.09
SMB(-1)	-0.08	-0.12	-0.17	-0.10	0.04	-0.03	-0.16	-0.13	-0.03	-0.10	-0.08	0.17	0.02
HML(-1)	-0.21	-0.15	-0.09	-0.33	-0.21	-0.26	-0.10	-0.17	-0.30	-0.31	-0.22	-0.18	-0.02

Table 18: Cross-autocorrelation coefficients – Jul1998-Jun2003
Table 18 shows the cross-autocorrelation coefficients of the portfolios under investigation. The (-1) indicates a lag of one in the calculations. The calculations are based on monthly returns. In the top line, SMALL, VALUE, and GROWTH are abbreviated and referred to as SML, VAL, and GRO, respectively.

In the second subperiod the low cross-autocorrelation between large growth stocks and small caps changes. More precisely, the second subsample period reveals a substantial shift in (cross-)autocorrelation relationships towards growth stocks. In fact, the coefficient for the cross-autocorrelation between BL_RF(-1) and SMALL_RF (SML_RF) jumps from 0.07 to 0.43. Further, the returns of all small cap portfolios seem to be lagging behind the returns of the large growth stocks. However, the period between Jul1998 and Jun2003 covers the time when tech stocks strongly outperformed the broad market. Hence, the dominant forecasting power of growth stocks for other portfolios could be due to the rally of the small tech stocks until around March 2000.

	BH_RF	BM_RF	BL_RF	SH_RF	SM_RF	SL_RF	MKT_RF	BIG_RF	SML_RF	VAL_RF	GRO_RF	SMB	HML
BH_RF(-1)	0.18	0.20	0.25	0.26	0.25	0.22	0.24	0.23	0.26	0.24	0.26	0.08	0.00
BM_RF(-1)	0.08	0.24	0.18	0.36	0.28	0.24	0.20	0.18	0.31	0.22	0.25	0.22	0.00
BL_RF(-1)	0.00	0.16	0.11	0.22	0.20	0.16	0.12	0.09	0.20	0.10	0.15	0.18	-0.05
SH_RF(-1)	-0.01	-0.04	-0.04	0.11	0.14	0.02	-0.05	-0.03	0.09	0.04	0.00	0.19	0.07
SM_RF(-1)	-0.08	-0.04	-0.03	0.10	0.08	-0.03	-0.04	-0.06	0.04	0.00	-0.04	0.16	0.05
SL_RF(-1)	-0.15	-0.05	-0.12	0.01	-0.06	-0.12	-0.12	-0.12	-0.07	-0.09	-0.14	0.08	0.06
MKT_RF(-1)	0.04	0.22	0.19	0.29	0.23	0.19	0.19	0.16	0.25	0.16	0.21	0.16	-0.04
BIG_RF(-1)	0.11	0.23	0.22	0.33	0.28	0.25	0.22	0.21	0.30	0.23	0.27	0.18	-0.01
SMALL_RF(-1)	-0.09	-0.05	-0.07	0.07	0.04	-0.06	-0.08	-0.08	0.01	-0.03	-0.07	0.15	0.06
VALUE_RF(-1)	0.11	0.10	0.14	0.22	0.23	0.16	0.13	0.13	0.21	0.17	0.17	0.14	0.03
GROWTH_RF(-1)	-0.11	0.03	-0.04	0.10	0.04	-0.02	-0.04	-0.05	0.03	-0.02	-0.03	0.13	0.02
SMB(-1)	-0.30	-0.39	-0.41	-0.34	-0.31	-0.41	-0.43	-0.41	-0.39	-0.35	-0.46	-0.01	0.11
HML(-1)	0.33	0.13	0.28	0.19	0.29	0.28	0.25	0.28	0.28	0.30	0.31	0.04	0.03

Table 19: Cross-autocorrelation coefficients – Jul2003-Jun2008
Table 19 shows the cross-autocorrelation coefficients of the portfolios under investigation. The (-1) indicates a lag of one in the calculations. The calculations are based on monthly returns. In the top line, SMALL, VALUE, and GROWTH are abbreviated and referred to as SML, VAL, and GRO, respectively.

The strong cross-autocorrelation between BL_RF(-1) and SML_RF reported above levels out during the third subsample period. However, the coefficient does not drop down to its earlier level. Interestingly, the coefficient of SMB(-1) increased sharply in absolute terms with respect to all long-only portfolios. In addition, SMB(-1) seems to lead other portfolios, with a negative sign on the coefficient. This negative sign of the coefficient seems puzzling, indicating a negative return of all long-only portfolios after months with positive long-short profits. I interpret this to mean that the relationship between the average small cap and the average large cap has been important in the (cross-)autocorrelation relationships since 2003. When the return of the average small cap deviates too much from the return of the average large cap, the aggregate market corrects in the following month. Small caps also correct, but the lower cross-autocorrelation coefficient indicates a somewhat weaker reaction. This is not related to a reverse movement of SMB as the autocorrelation coefficient with magnitude around zero indicates.

Overall, the three subsample periods can be summarized as follows. The first period, Jul1993-Jun1998, was marked by a high leading power of large caps, in particular large value stocks. Primarily, the returns of small caps seem to be lead by returns of large caps. This result is in line with previous findings for the US market, as documented in the literature. The second period, Jul1998-Jun2003, which covers the tech rally, revealed substantial leads of growth stocks. This might be due to the strong autocorrelation in returns of growth stocks during that time. In the third period, Jul2003-Jun2008, the returns of the long-short portfolio SMB seem to lead returns of size as well as book-to-market sorted portfolios.

In the following, I compare the above-estimated cross-serial correlations to the implied cross-serial correlations which, according to Boudoukh, Richardson and Whitelaw (1994), can be calculated as

$$(36) \qquad corr(R_{it}, R_{jt-1}) = corr(R_{it}, R_{jt}) \cdot corr(R_{it}, R_{it-1}).$$

The implied cross-autocorrelation $corr(R_{it}, R_{jt-1})$ between the returns of two portfolios i and j is the product of the contemporaneous correlation $corr(R_{it}, R_{jt})$ between i and j and the autocorrelation of the returns of portfolio i. However, Boudoukh, Richardson, and Whitelaw (1994) report differences between the implied and the empirical cross-autocorrelations which are attributed to estimation errors.

I subsequently quantify these differences for the sample and subsample periods. In order to keep the analysis brief, I directly report the differences between the estimated cross-autocorrelations and the implied cross-autocorrelations instead of documenting both values separately.

	BH_RF	BM_RF	BL_RF	SH_RF	SM_RF	SL_RF	MKT_RF	BIG_RF	SML_RF	VAL_RF	GRO_RF	SMB	HML
BH_RF(-1)	0.01	0.08	0.16	0.22	0.14	0.19	0.12	0.05	0.17	0.10	0.19	0.20	-0.06
BM_RF(-1)	0.05	0.00	0.02	0.24	0.08	0.13	-0.01	-0.04	0.12	0.12	0.08	0.27	-0.02
BL_RF(-1)	0.09	0.11	0.00	0.19	0.09	0.08	-0.01	0.01	0.09	0.12	0.02	0.12	0.01
SH_RF(-1)	-0.06	-0.02	-0.08	0.00	0.05	0.03	-0.09	-0.10	-0.04	-0.11	-0.02	0.19	-0.04
SM_RF(-1)	0.00	0.03	-0.01	0.19	0.00	0.08	-0.03	-0.04	0.04	0.06	0.04	0.23	0.00
SL_RF(-1)	0.00	-0.03	-0.04	0.13	0.02	0.00	-0.06	-0.07	0.00	0.03	-0.01	0.21	-0.08
MKT_RF(-1)	0.08	0.10	0.02	0.21	0.09	0.10	0.00	0.01	0.10	0.12	0.04	0.15	0.00
BIG_RF(-1)	0.06	0.07	0.07	0.25	0.12	0.16	0.04	0.00	0.15	0.13	0.12	0.24	-0.03
SMALL_RF(-1)	-0.02	-0.01	-0.05	0.13	0.02	0.04	-0.07	-0.08	0.00	0.00	0.00	0.24	-0.05
VALUE_RF(-1)	-0.03	0.04	0.06	0.14	0.11	0.14	0.03	-0.02	0.09	0.00	0.11	0.23	-0.06
GROWTH_RF(-1)	0.04	0.03	-0.03	0.17	0.06	0.04	-0.05	-0.04	0.04	0.08	0.00	0.20	-0.05
SMB(-1)	-0.11	-0.12	-0.18	-0.19	-0.14	-0.18	-0.17	-0.12	-0.22	-0.19	-0.18	0.00	-0.03
HML(-1)	-0.10	0.01	0.12	-0.07	0.07	0.13	0.11	0.03	0.06	-0.11	0.14	0.01	0.00

Table 20: Differences between estimated and implied cross-autocorrelations – Jul1993-Jun2008
Table 20 presents the differences between the estimated cross-serial correlations and the implied cross-serial correlations. The sample period ranges from Jul1993 to Jun2008. The implied cross-serial correlations are calculated by $corr(R_{it}, R_{jt-1}) = corr(R_{it}, R_{jt}) \cdot corr(R_{it}, R_{it-1})$.

As can be seen from Table 20, the differences between estimated and implied cross-autocorrelations are often considerable. Note that positive values indicate higher estimated coefficients than implied coefficients. An interesting observation is the asymmetry between the differences among certain portfolios. For instance, consider the values in the row BIG_RF(-1). The values 0.25, 0.12, and 0.16 in the intersections between BIG_RF(-1) and SH_RF, SM_RF, and SL_RF are all positive. In the following row marked SMALL_RF(-1) consider the intersections between SMALL_RF(-1) and BH_RF, BM_RF, and BL_RF. The values -0.02, -0.01, and -0.05 are all negative. Hence, in the case in which the returns of BIG_RF are considered as leading, the estimated cross-autocorrelations are higher than the implied coefficients. The opposite is true for the cases where the returns of SMALL_RF are considered as leaders. This tendency is consistent with the values reported in Boudoukh, Richardson, and Whitelaw (1994), but their differences are much lower than the ones presented above. However, the applied estimation method of the autocorrelation and cross-autocorrelation coefficients differs from that of Boudoukh, Richardson, and Whitelaw (1994) with respect to the application of overlapping return periods. This might explain the differences to some extent. Nevertheless, it seems implausible that different estimation procedures can account for the entire difference. Consider, for instance, the relationship of BH_RF(-1) and SH_RF. The difference between the estimated and the implied cross-autocorrelation is 0.22. For the opposite relationship SH_RF(-1) and BH_RF the difference amounts to -0.06. In the first case the estimated value is 0.22 higher than the implied value, but in the second case the estimated value is 0.06 lower than the implied value. As all estimated and implied cross-serial correlations for these portfolios are positive, the idea of general overestimation of cross-autocorrelations thus seems unappealing. Rather, the data suggests an overestimation of cross-serial correlation if large caps are used as leaders and an underestimation if small caps are used as leaders. This insight leads me toward a cautious interpretation of the differences between estimated and implied cross-serial correlations.

	BH_RF	BM_RF	BL_RF	SH_RF	SM_RF	SL_RF	MKT_RF	BIG_RF	SML_RF	VAL_RF	GRO_RF	SMB	HML
BH_RF(-1)	0.01	0.26	0.30	0.31	0.37	0.42	0.30	0.19	0.38	0.21	0.40	0.20	0.13
BM_RF(-1)	0.10	0.01	0.11	0.19	0.05	0.00	0.11	-0.04	0.04	0.13	0.06	0.03	0.20
BL_RF(-1)	0.12	-0.02	0.00	0.04	0.01	-0.08	-0.01	-0.12	-0.08	0.05	-0.06	-0.01	0.17
SH_RF(-1)	-0.13	0.04	0.03	0.01	0.08	0.07	0.02	-0.12	-0.03	-0.19	0.06	0.10	0.03
SM_RF(-1)	0.01	0.07	-0.02	0.19	0.02	0.13	-0.01	-0.08	0.07	0.06	0.06	0.17	0.14
SL_RF(-1)	0.06	0.10	0.08	0.11	0.08	0.00	0.08	0.00	-0.01	0.05	0.07	-0.04	-0.02
MKT_RF(-1)	0.12	-0.02	0.01	0.05	0.01	-0.08	0.00	-0.12	-0.07	0.05	-0.06	-0.01	0.19
BIG_RF(-1)	0.09	0.10	0.16	0.22	0.17	0.13	0.16	0.01	0.13	0.15	0.15	0.09	0.21
SMALL_RF(-1)	-0.02	0.08	0.03	0.12	0.07	0.08	0.04	-0.08	0.01	-0.03	0.07	0.09	0.05
VALUE_RF(-1)	-0.07	0.18	0.19	0.19	0.27	0.30	0.20	0.04	0.21	0.01	0.27	0.18	0.10
GROWTH_RF(-1)	0.10	0.05	0.04	0.08	0.05	-0.05	0.04	-0.07	-0.05	0.05	0.00	-0.03	0.09
SMB(-1)	-0.17	-0.03	-0.17	-0.13	-0.15	-0.07	-0.17	-0.12	-0.18	-0.26	-0.11	0.00	-0.21
HML(-1)	-0.21	0.15	0.17	0.12	0.26	0.41	0.18	0.14	0.32	-0.05	0.32	0.26	0.00

Table 21: Differences between estimated and implied cross-autocorrelations – Jul1993-Jun1998
Table 21 presents the differences between the estimated cross-serial correlations and the implied cross-serial correlations. The sample period ranges from Jul1993 to Jun1998. The implied cross-serial correlations are calculated by $corr(R_{it}, R_{jt-1}) = corr(R_{it}, R_{jt}) \cdot corr(R_{it}, R_{it-1})$.

Table 21 depicts the differences of the estimated and the implied cross-serial correlations for the first subsample period. Some deviations seem quite strong but, due to a smaller sample, the results have to be interpreted and compared carefully. However, comparing the values from Table 21 to the values of the second subsample period, which are presented below, might be more appropriate than a comparison to the findings concerning the full sample period.

For the sake of brevity I restrict the comparison between the subsample periods to the two basic styles BIG and SMALL, which also seem symptomatic for other relationships. With respect to BIG_RF(-1) and SMALL_RF, the same order for all subperiods holds. The estimated cross-autocorrelations exceed the implied cross-autocorrelations. The opposite holds for SMALL_RF(-1) and BIG_RF, where the implied coefficients are larger than the estimated coefficients.

	BH_RF	BM_RF	BL_RF	SH_RF	SM_RF	SL_RF	MKT_RF	BIG_RF	SML_RF	VAL_RF	GRO_RF	SMB	HML
BH_RF(-1)	0.01	0.04	0.02	0.18	0.00	0.11	0.00	0.01	0.05	0.06	0.07	0.29	-0.14
BM_RF(-1)	0.07	0.01	-0.11	0.25	0.00	0.08	-0.10	-0.05	0.03	0.12	0.00	0.40	-0.06
BL_RF(-1)	0.14	0.21	0.02	0.34	0.12	0.14	0.05	0.12	0.14	0.22	0.07	0.22	-0.07
SH_RF(-1)	0.03	0.01	-0.17	0.01	0.04	0.06	-0.14	-0.06	-0.07	-0.06	-0.03	0.28	-0.09
SM_RF(-1)	0.12	0.09	0.01	0.29	0.00	0.12	0.01	0.06	0.07	0.18	0.09	0.31	-0.06
SL_RF(-1)	0.10	-0.01	-0.09	0.22	0.04	0.01	-0.09	-0.03	0.00	0.13	-0.02	0.38	-0.10
MKT_RF(-1)	0.13	0.17	-0.01	0.33	0.09	0.14	0.02	0.08	0.13	0.20	0.06	0.27	-0.08
BIG_RF(-1)	0.08	0.08	-0.04	0.28	0.03	0.12	-0.03	0.01	0.07	0.14	0.05	0.35	-0.10
SMALL_RF(-1)	0.10	0.03	-0.09	0.22	0.03	0.06	-0.08	-0.01	0.00	0.11	0.01	0.39	-0.10
VALUE_RF(-1)	0.02	0.03	-0.07	0.13	0.01	0.10	-0.07	-0.02	0.00	0.01	0.04	0.33	-0.14
GROWTH_RF(-1)	0.13	0.08	-0.06	0.29	0.08	0.06	-0.04	0.03	0.06	0.18	0.02	0.36	-0.10
SMB(-1)	0.03	-0.08	-0.08	-0.12	-0.01	-0.10	-0.08	-0.03	-0.12	-0.06	-0.06	0.00	0.02
HML(-1)	-0.19	-0.09	0.00	-0.33	-0.11	0.02	-0.02	-0.08	-0.10	-0.29	0.01	-0.17	0.00

Table 22: Differences between estimated and implied cross-autocorrelations – Jul1998-Jun2003
Table 22 presents the differences between the estimated cross-serial correlations and the implied cross-serial correlations. The sample period ranges from Jul1998 to Jun2003. The implied cross-serial correlations are calculated by $corr(R_{it}, R_{jt-1}) = corr(R_{it}, R_{jt}) \cdot corr(R_{it}, R_{it-1})$.

Table 22 presents the differences between the estimated and the implied cross-autocorrelations for the second subsample period, and Table 23 displays the results for the sample period which covers the data from Jul2003 to Jun2008. As mentioned before, the patterns among BIG and SMALL hold for all subperiods. However, the differences are low for the second subsample period.

	BH_RF	BM_RF	BL_RF	SH_RF	SM_RF	SL_RF	MKT_RF	BIG_RF	SML_RF	VAL_RF	GRO_RF	SMB	HML
BH_RF(-1)	0.02	0.05	0.20	0.20	0.19	0.30	0.12	0.07	0.25	0.09	0.29	0.08	-0.01
BM_RF(-1)	-0.03	0.02	0.11	0.30	0.23	0.32	0.04	0.01	0.30	0.10	0.27	0.22	0.00
BL_RF(-1)	-0.09	0.00	0.00	0.16	0.15	0.22	-0.05	-0.06	0.19	0.00	0.18	0.18	-0.05
SH_RF(-1)	-0.11	-0.19	-0.10	0.00	0.08	0.11	-0.17	-0.17	0.08	-0.09	0.03	0.20	0.06
SM_RF(-1)	-0.19	-0.19	-0.09	0.01	0.00	0.07	-0.16	-0.20	0.03	-0.13	-0.01	0.17	0.04
SL_RF(-1)	-0.25	-0.19	-0.18	-0.06	-0.12	0.00	-0.23	-0.25	-0.08	-0.21	-0.11	0.08	0.06
MKT_RF(-1)	-0.07	0.03	0.09	0.22	0.18	0.26	0.01	-0.01	0.24	0.04	0.24	0.15	-0.04
BIG_RF(-1)	-0.03	0.03	0.13	0.26	0.23	0.33	0.06	0.02	0.29	0.09	0.29	0.18	-0.02
SMALL_RF(-1)	-0.21	-0.20	-0.14	-0.02	-0.03	0.06	-0.21	-0.23	0.00	-0.16	-0.04	0.15	0.06
VALUE_RF(-1)	-0.04	-0.06	0.08	0.13	0.16	0.24	-0.01	-0.03	0.20	0.01	0.19	0.14	0.02
GROWTH_RF(-1)	-0.22	-0.14	-0.13	0.02	-0.02	0.09	-0.19	-0.21	0.02	-0.15	0.00	0.13	0.02
SMB(-1)	-0.27	-0.34	-0.39	-0.37	-0.34	-0.36	-0.39	-0.36	-0.39	-0.36	-0.46	0.00	0.11
HML(-1)	0.24	0.10	0.29	0.17	0.28	0.26	0.25	0.23	0.28	0.23	0.30	0.04	0.00

Table 23: Differences between estimated and implied cross-autocorrelations – Jul2003-Jun2008
Table 23 presents the differences between the estimated cross-serial correlations and the implied cross-serial correlations. The sample period ranges from Jul2003 to Jun2008. The implied cross-serial correlations are calculated by $corr(R_{it}, R_{jt-1}) = corr(R_{it}, R_{jt}) \cdot corr(R_{it}, R_{it-1})$.

The lead-lag relationship between large caps and small caps might be the one most frequently considered in the literature. The evidence presented above confirms this relationship for the Swiss stock market. Moreover, the formation of the combined style portfolios allows for a more detailed investigation of lead-lag relationships. As the analyses of the subsample periods indicate, there are more and even stronger lead-lag relationships among other portfolios.

Boudoukh, Richardson, and Whitelaw (1994) argue that not cross-serial correlation but serial correlation itself matters. Moreover, cross-autocorrelations can be calculated by using contemporaneous correlations and autocorrelations. However, the above calculations show considerable differences between empirical cross-serial correlations and implied cross-serial correlations. Estimation errors could be a reason for these differences. Another reason might be that empirical cross-autocorrelations carry information which cannot be captured by contemporaneous correlations and autocorrelations. Due to the magnitude and structure of the differences, I find the latter argument the more appealing one. Hence, besides autocorrelations, I also consider cross-autocorrelations in the following model-building process.

6.2. Basic Forecasting Models

The above evidence on serial and cross-serial correlation suggests forecasting possibilities which could be exploited by investment strategies. The idea is simple. I use past returns in order to forecast future returns. The simplest forecasting models consist of two variables, one which is forecasted and one which serves as predictor. In the cases below, both variables are returns. Thus, first of all, it has to be determined which returns are to be forecasted and which returns can take the role of a predictor variable. This issue is addressed in the present section. However, this section focuses on the basic ideas of the forecasting models and will provide some intuition. The specific models which are applied in the investment strategies are presented along the description of the respective strategy.

In order to determine those variables which will be forecasted, I assume an investor who has an Investment Opportunity Set (IOS) of the six Fama-French Portfolios SH, SM, SL, BH, BM, BL, the four styles SMALL, BIG, VALUE, GROWTH, plus MKT.

This means that the investor considers the market segments mentioned and decides to invest in one of those segments. Moreover, the investor does not invest in more than one market segment portfolio at the same time.

The outlined IOS represents the portfolios for which the returns will be forecasted. The more difficult question is which returns will be used as predictor variables. Basically, I consider two possibilities which can be described by the following two equations.

(37) $$y_t = \alpha + \phi_1 y_{t-k} + \varepsilon_t$$

(38) $$y_t = \alpha + \phi_2 x_{t-k} + \varepsilon_t$$

In (37) the return y of a portfolio in month t is forecasted by a constant α plus ϕ_1 times the lagged return of portfolio y. In (38) the return y of a portfolio in month t is forecasted by a constant α plus ϕ_2 times the lagged return of another portfolio x.

Besides the decision about the lag-structure, there are more questions which have to be addressed in the same turn. First, there may be changes in the predictive power of the portfolios. Hence, the predictor variable should be changed over time. Furthermore, the parameter ϕ_i might change over time as well. Therefore, it may be appropriate to calibrate the model several times instead of once at the beginning. With respect to calibration new issues arise. One has to determine the calibration period. For example, it may be more accurate to apply a short calibration period in order to account for the more recent past. However, a shorter calibration window also has its drawbacks such as larger estimation errors. In addition, the calibration window can be a fixed rolling one or a growing one where the calibration period is increased as more and more data becomes available.

Another crucial issue in forecasting is data availability. It is inappropriate to forecast returns with calibrations estimated by using the entire sample data as these data might not have been available to the investor by the time of the investment decision. For example, consider an investor in Jun1998 who wishes to forecast the return for

Jul1998. His forecast should clearly not be based on a model which was calibrated by using the data from Jul 1993 to Jun2008 as the data as of Jul1998 would not have been available to the investor in Jun1998. Hence, depending on the calibration period, the test period for the investment strategies is limited to only a part of the full sample period. In other words, the testing procedure described, which is based on an investor with information up to a certain point in time, may be interpreted as an out-of-sample test. However, besides investigating investment strategies which are based on an in-sample calibration, an out-of-sample test can be done statistically as well. In order to keep the analysis brief, I restrict the reported results to those of the investment strategies.

As a starting point, I use the above evidence on serial correlations and cross-autocorrelations in order to build the models. The most promising forecasting models might be those which are based on high autocorrelation or high cross-serial correlation. As outlined in section 5.3.1. serial correlation is most apparent at lag one. Thus, the subsequent models use returns with a lag of one month as predictor variables. Moreover, I run several investment strategies which have changing calibration windows and predictor variables in order to account for time-varying characteristics.

y(t)	y(t-1) / x(t-1)	Constant	Coefficient	R^2
	Jul1993-Jun1998			
BH_RF	BH_RF(-1)	0.009	0.401	16.9%
BM_RF	BH_RF(-1)	0.008	0.329	10.2%
BL_RF	BH_RF(-1)	0.013	0.271	6.5%
SH_RF	BH_RF(-1)	0.007	0.334	10.7%
SM_RF	BH_RF(-1)	0.005	0.455	23.6%
SL_RF	BH_RF(-1)	0.005	0.467	20.5%
MKT_RF	BH_RF(-1)	0.012	0.277	7.6%
BIG_RF	BH_RF(-1)	0.010	0.334	15.5%
SMALL_RF	BH_RF(-1)	0.006	0.420	23.8%
VALUE_RF	BH_RF(-1)	0.009	0.369	19.4%
GROWTH_RF	BH_RF(-1)	0.009	0.371	15.8%

Table 24: Examples of calibrated forecasting models
The above table presents results from regression analyses of the form:

$$y_t = \alpha + \phi y_{t-1} + \varepsilon_t$$

or

$$y_t = \alpha + \phi x_{t-1} + \varepsilon_t$$

The returns of the portfolios listed in the column y(t) were regressed on the lagged returns of the portfolios listed in the column y(t-1) / x(t-1) plus a constant. (-1) indicates that returns of the predictor variables were lagged one month. The calibration window ranges from Jul1993 to Jun1998. The fifth column contains the values of the R-squared measure.

Before creating and evaluating investment strategies, I intend to clarify some steps. Table 24 will help to exemplify the calibration and model-building process. The portfolios listed in the column y(t) represent the IOS. The portfolios listed in the column y(t-1) / x(t-1) contain the predictor variables. The predictor variables are chosen according to the coefficients of the cross-autocorrelations shown in Table 17. The highest (cross-)autocorrelation coefficient determines the predictor portfolio. For instance, the cross-serial correlation between BM_RF and BH_RF(-1) is 0.32. This is the highest value in the column of BM_RF in Table 17. Thus, the excess returns of portfolio BH are applied in order to predict the excess returns of portfolio BM. Moreover, as we can see from the above table and Table 17, BH seems to be a strong predictor as it is leading all other portfolios during the first subsample period. This seems to be a supportive argument for the interpretation that serial correlation is at the heart of cross-autocorrelations. Now, the calibrations shown in Table 24 can be used to forecast the returns of Jul1998. The investment strategies that arise will be exploited later. First, I show some possible refinements of the forecasting models which may be of interest in practice.

6.3. Robustness and Possible Refinements

As outlined in the literature review, there may be other effects which might be linked to style investing and could be of interest with respect to forecasting. One such effect is the observation of calendar anomalies. Especially with the returns of small cap portfolios in view, this effect may be relevant. For instance, Keim (1983) finds small caps to having large abnormal returns in January. Hence, the basic models reported above might be enriched with a January variable to improve forecasting power.

Portfolio	January	February	March	April	May	June	July	August	September	October	November	December
	Jul1993-Jun1998											
BH_RF	0.04	0.04	0.01	0.01	0.03	0.01	0.02	0.00	-0.01	0.03	0.02	0.02
	2.05	*1.91*	*0.32*	*0.51*	*1.26*	*0.35*	*0.96*	*-0.05*	*-0.28*	*1.45*	*0.90*	*1.23*
BM_RF	0.03	0.01	0.02	0.01	0.03	0.01	0.00	-0.01	0.02	-0.01	0.03	0.02
	1.66	*0.61*	*1.00*	*0.57*	*1.69*	*0.50*	*-0.08*	*-0.31*	*0.81*	*-0.53*	*1.26*	*1.09*
BL_RF	0.05	0.02	0.00	0.00	0.02	0.01	-0.02	0.01	0.01	0.01	0.04	0.04
	2.40	*1.12*	*0.21*	*0.06*	*0.73*	*0.68*	*-0.87*	*0.55*	*0.46*	*0.34*	*1.92*	*2.16*
SH_RF	0.02	0.04	0.00	0.01	0.05	-0.01	0.00	0.02	-0.02	0.00	0.02	0.05
	0.85	*2.01*	*-0.02*	*0.38*	*2.68*	*-0.78*	*0.13*	*1.11*	*-1.25*	*-0.03*	*1.14*	*2.49*
SM_RF	0.03	0.03	0.04	0.02	0.02	0.01	0.00	0.00	0.00	-0.02	0.01	0.02
	1.40	*1.54*	*2.19*	*1.20*	*1.12*	*0.52*	*-0.11*	*-0.07*	*0.24*	*-1.09*	*0.48*	*1.33*
SL_RF	0.03	-0.01	0.04	0.01	0.03	0.01	0.01	0.02	0.00	-0.01	0.01	0.04
	1.35	*-0.60*	*1.94*	*0.62*	*1.28*	*0.54*	*0.45*	*1.14*	*-0.20*	*-0.63*	*0.33*	*1.85*
MKT_RF	0.05	0.02	0.01	0.00	0.02	0.01	-0.02	0.01	0.01	0.01	0.04	0.04
	2.40	*1.19*	*0.32*	*0.12*	*0.91*	*0.72*	*-0.82*	*0.48*	*0.53*	*0.33*	*1.91*	*2.15*
BIG_RF	0.04	0.03	0.01	0.01	0.03	0.01	0.00	0.00	0.01	0.01	0.03	0.03
	2.49	*1.49*	*0.64*	*0.47*	*1.50*	*0.63*	*0.03*	*0.11*	*0.42*	*0.53*	*1.67*	*1.83*
SMALL_RF	0.02	0.02	0.03	0.01	0.03	0.00	0.00	0.01	-0.01	-0.01	0.01	0.04
	1.37	*1.08*	*1.59*	*0.84*	*1.92*	*0.13*	*0.20*	*0.85*	*-0.44*	*-0.65*	*0.75*	*2.15*
VALUE_RF	0.03	0.04	0.00	0.01	0.04	0.00	0.01	0.01	-0.01	0.01	0.02	0.04
	1.81	*2.38*	*0.21*	*0.55*	*2.37*	*-0.23*	*0.69*	*0.62*	*-0.90*	*0.92*	*1.24*	*2.24*
GROWTH_RF	0.04	0.01	0.02	0.01	0.02	0.01	0.00	0.02	0.00	0.00	0.02	0.04
	2.08	*0.31*	*1.19*	*0.39*	*1.10*	*0.68*	*-0.22*	*0.95*	*0.15*	*-0.14*	*1.26*	*2.22*

Table 25: Calendar anomalies
Table 25 presents potential monthly seasonalities. The portfolio returns between Jul1993 and Jun1998 were regressed on dummy variables for each month without including a constant. The numbers in the same line as the dependent variable represent the values of the coefficients corresponding to the months in the top line. Numbers in italics represent the respective T-values.

Table 25 presents results for calendar anomalies. Instead of testing for an isolated January effect, I test whether other months show significant returns as well. With our investor in Jun1998 in mind, I use the sample period Jul1993 to Jun1998 for the estimates. The coefficients can be interpreted as the average return of the listed portfolios in the respective month. The table above shows mixed evidence on the

January effect. Interestingly, no significant January effect can be observed for the small cap portfolios. In contrast, some of the large caps portfolios exhibit high average returns in January. Moreover, the most significant average returns can be found in December. However, the sample period is limited to 60 observations. Hence, the results have to be interpreted with caution. Nevertheless, given the evidence in the literature, an investor might think about including a calendar variable in his forecasting model.

Another refinement is to account for extreme observations. This is interesting for several reasons. On the one hand, extreme observations might distort the forecasting models. Thus, the isolation of this effect is important in order to check whether the forecasting models are powerful just because of a few outliers. On the other hand, I hypothesise that unusually high returns, for example, returns greater than two standard deviations from zero, contain important information with respect to forecasting power. Therefore, an isolation of such an effect may improve the forecasting models.

Based on the data of the first subsample period, I run regression analyses in order to check for an extreme observations effect. In order to test for the influence of extreme observations, a new dummy variable is introduced. The variable takes the value 1 if the observation is greater than two standard deviations from zero. The variable takes the value 0 if the observation is within a two-sigma bound.

y(t)	y(t-1) / x(t-1)	Constant	Coefficient	2-Sigma	Adj. R^2
		Jul1993-Jun1998			
BH_RF	BH_RF(-1)	0.010	0.438	-0.023	15.8%
BM_RF	BH_RF(-1)	0.008	0.317	0.007	7.2%
BL_RF	BH_RF(-1)	0.012	0.255	0.010	3.4%
SH_RF	BH_RF(-1)	0.007	0.325	0.006	7.6%
SM_RF	BH_RF(-1)	0.004	0.411	0.026	23.4%
SL_RF	BH_RF(-1)	0.005	0.454	0.008	17.9%
MKT_RF	BH_RF(-1)	0.012	0.261	0.010	4.6%
BIG_RF	BH_RF(-1)	0.011	0.337	-0.002	12.5%
SMALL_RF	BH_RF(-1)	0.006	0.398	0.013	21.9%
VALUE_RF	BH_RF(-1)	0.009	0.383	-0.009	16.9%
GROWTH_RF	BH_RF(-1)	0.009	0.356	0.009	13.0%

Table 26: Effect of extreme observations
The above table presents results from regression analyses. The returns of the portfolios listed in the column y(t) are regressed on the lagged returns of the portfolios listed in the column y(t-1) / x(t-1) plus a constant plus a dummy variable dum_{t-1} for extreme observations. (-1) indicates that returns of the predictor variables are lagged one month. Depending on the lagged predictor variable the regressions are of the form:

$$y_t = \alpha + \phi_1 y_{t-1} + \lambda_1 dum_{t-1} + \varepsilon_t$$

or

$$y_t = \alpha + \phi_2 x_{t-1} + \lambda_2 dum_{t-1} + \varepsilon_t$$

The dummy variable takes a value of one if the absolute observed return is greater than two standard deviations. The time period for the calculation of the standard deviation equals the subsample period. The column marked Coefficient contains the values of ϕ_i which refer to y_{t-1} or x_{t-1}, respectively. The column 2-Sigma contains the values of the coefficient λ_i. The last column contains the values of the adjusted R-squared measure.

Table 26 exhibits information about the effect of extreme observations on the explanatory power of the forecasting models. The basic models (37) and (38) are extended by a dummy variable which accounts for observations greater than two standard deviations.

(39) $$y_t = \alpha + \phi_1 y_{t-1} + \lambda_1 dum_{t-1} + \varepsilon_t$$

(40) $$y_t = \alpha + \phi_2 x_{t-1} + \lambda_2 dum_{t-1} + \varepsilon_t$$

In (39) the return y of a portfolio in month t is forecasted by a constant α plus ϕ_1 times the lagged return of portfolio y plus λ_1 times 1 if the last observation is greater than two standard deviations. In (40) the return y of a portfolio in month t is forecasted by a constant α plus ϕ_2 times the lagged return of another portfolio x plus λ_2 times 1 if the last observation is greater than two standard deviations.

A comparison of adjusted R-squared measures from Table 26 to the R-squared measures of Table 24 reveals no additional forecasting power of extreme observations. As before, the analysis is based on the first subsample period. Hence, an investor might check again for explanatory power of extreme observations as more data is available to him.

Given the information and evidence from above, an investor in Jun1998 might decide to apply the simplest model considered so far in order to create his investment strategy. Thus, the following investment strategies are based on the most parsimonious models which may be also an advantage in keeping the explanations as clear as possible. A real-world investor might check for calendar anomalies or the effect of extreme observations when new data is available. Moreover, other specifications of extreme observations could be tested. Furthermore, there is the possibility of applying various different time intervals for the estimation of the standard deviations; however, this is beyond the scope of my research.

7. Empirical Part II – Investment Strategies

7.1. Hypothesis II

A passive buy and hold portfolio outperforms investment strategies which use the returns of the Fama-French factor-mimicking Portfolios or of components of these portfolios as predictors.

Cochrane (1999b) points out the possible application of market timing strategies as a main implication of return predictability. Hence, the rejection of the random walk model might reveal exploitable investment strategies. Moreover, investment strategies can shed light on the economic significance of forecasting power. The findings above support the evidence on return predictability; however, nothing was said about the economic magnitude and its meaning for portfolio management. How a market timing strategy based on the previous analyses might look may be of interest to practitioners. Hence, I identify two reasons for a test of the above-stated hypothesis. First, there is the economic significance which is of interest. The second reason is the possible uncertainty about statistical tests of forecasting models. For instance, Leitch and Tanner (1991) or Gerlow, Irwin and Liu (1993) show a possible economic success of forecasting models even if statistical measures do not support their predictive power.

7.2. Overview

The investment strategies which are developed and evaluated below in sections 7.5. and 7.6. are based on the forecasting models described in section 6.2. The above evidence suggests building parsimonious models with respect to the available data at Jun1993. This is the starting point of the development of the investment strategies shown in later sections.

Before developing the investment strategies, I introduce some calibration concepts in the following section. The calibration of the forecasting models is a crucial issue as there are many possible calibration procedures such as, for instance, rolling or recursive approaches.

Another important aspect with investment strategies is their evaluation. The success of an investment strategy is usually measured by its performance. However, today there is a wide range of performance measurement concepts available. Thus, I briefly outline the performance measurement concepts in section 7.4. which I apply later in order to evaluate the investment strategies.

7.3. Calibration Windows and Investment Process

With respect to the calibration procedure, a variety of combinations is possible. Basically, two questions have to be addressed. The first regards the length of the calibration window, i.e., how much historical data will be used in order to calibrate the model. The second one concerns the re-estimation frequency, i.e., how many times the model is to be re-calibrated. For instance, one could chose a formation period of 48 months and apply a monthly rolling window. This means that a calibration window of 48 months is used to estimate the parameters and after each month the estimation window is moved one month. An alternative approach would be to apply a recursive window with a formation period which starts with 60 months. There are numerous alternatives that are applicable. Hence, it seems almost impossible to test all possible combinations.

In order to keep the analyses consistent with previous analyses, the calibration period is set to 60 months, which equals the length of the subsample periods. This choice is also consistent with the calibration windows applied by Arshanapalli, Switzer, and Panju (2007). However, as noted above, a calibration window can be fixed, rolling, or recursive. A fixed calibration window means that the model parameters are estimated once and then used throughout the sample. In other words, with a fixed calibration window, the parameters will not be updated as time passes. Rolling and recursive windows are a little more labour intensive. A rolling window means re-estimating the model parameters at a certain interval with a fixed number of past observations. For example, an investor could re-estimate his model each month with the data of the last 60 months. A recursive window keeps the first observation constant, while the last observation is updated; thus, a recursive window uses a growing number of observations for the parameterisation. For example, an investor could start with a calibration of 60 months and re-estimate the parameters every month, which means that he would use 61 months of data after the following month and 62 months two months after the starting point.

The calibration of the forecasting models is the starting point of the investment process as the estimated parameters are used to forecast the next month's return. Based on this forecast, an investment decision is made and the investor allocates his funds to the most promising portfolio. At the end of the process comes the evaluation of how successful the applied investment strategy was.

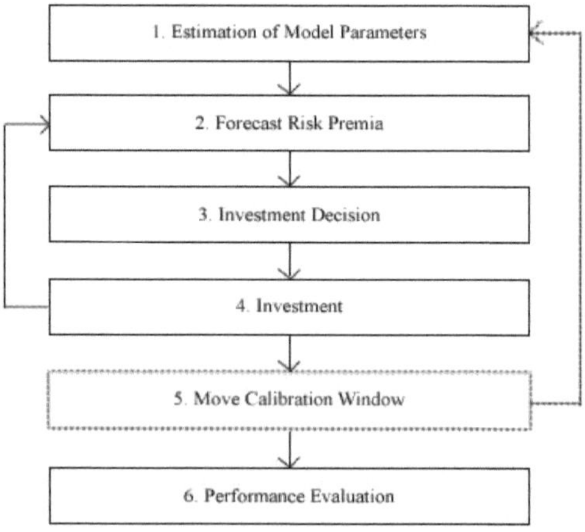

Figure 6: Investment process
The above investment process follows Schnedler (2003, p. 102) and consists of six steps. The solid lines represent steps which are performed for every strategy. The dotted lines mark necessary actions for rolling and recursive window calibrations.

Figure 6 illustrates the general investment approach. Depending on the calibration window, there are five or six steps. In the following, each of the steps is outlined in more detail.

1. Estimation of Model Parameters: As indicated above, the first step is to estimate the model parameters in order to forecast the returns. The parameters are estimated with data from 60 months. The window is either fixed, rolling, or recursive.

2. Forecast Returns: The estimated parameters and the returns of the leading portfolios are used to forecast the next month's returns of each of the portfolios in the investment opportunity set.

3. Investment Decision: The investment criterion is the forecasted return. Depending on the definition of the investment strategy, taking positions in a fixed income asset may be allowed if all forecasted risk premia are negative.

4. Investment: A long position in the portfolio with the highest forecasted return or in the fixed income asset is taken and held for one month. At the end of the month the next month's risk premia are forecasted.

5. Move Calibration Window: If a rolling or recursive window is applied, the calibration window needs to be shifted or extended by one observation. This restarts the process as new model parameters have to be estimated.

6. Performance Evaluation: At the end of the investment horizon, the performance of each strategy is evaluated. All performance measures are provided before any transaction costs. Brokerage costs are in practice highly heterogeneous among investors. While institutional investors might have substantial negotiation power to keep costs low, private investors might strongly reduce their performance by frequently transacting. However, other transactions costs such as bid/ask spreads are more difficult to account for and strongly linked to market microstructure issues (Grinold and Kahn (1995, pp. 291-294)).

7.4. Performance Measurement

There are many ways to evaluate investment strategies. This section is intended to provide an overview of a number of frequently applied performance measures. Additionally, more recent ideas regarding performance evaluation will be outlined.

The Sharpe Ratio published by Sharpe (1966) is one of the most famous performance measures. The ratio is based on the idea of the Capital Market Line (CML). The higher the slope of the CML, the higher the return per unit of risk is. Within Modern Portfolio Theory, the market portfolio is the tangential portfolio of the CML. Hence, the market portfolio has the highest reward per unit of standard deviation. The slope of the ex-post CML is the Sharpe Ratio. The ratio is widely used in practice. Sharpe (1994) identified many advantages to it over other performance measures. Cochrane (1999b) suggests the Sharpe ratio as a good performance measure for market timing strategies. Formally, the ratio is defined as below:

(41) $$SR(P) = \frac{R_P - R_0}{\sigma_P}$$

$R_P - R_0$ is the risk premium. The risk premium is divided by the risk σ_P, i.e., the standard deviation, of the portfolio returns. It is common to evaluate the ratio over an annual investment horizon. Two aspects are important: First, the rate of the risk free asset influences the ratio, which might be relevant for international comparisons. Second, the ratio depends on the time period. The return in the numerator is proportional to the time, while the standard deviation in the denominator grows proportionally to the square root of time.

The so-called Treynor Ratio follows a similar approach (Treynor (1965)). Instead of the standard deviation, which covers systematic and unsystematic risk, the Treynor Ratio applies the systematic risk only.

(42) $$TR(P) = \frac{R_P - R_0}{\beta_P}$$

The excess return $R_P - R_0$ is divided by the Beta β_P of the portfolio. In other words, the Treynor Ratio measures the excess return which corresponds to a Beta of 1. However, to calculate Beta, a benchmark is necessary, i.e., the ratio is not benchmark free. Roll (1978) as well as Lehmann and Modest (1987) show a serious effect on the judgement of investment strategies when different benchmarks are used.

A performance measure which has also attracted much attention in practice is Jensen's Alpha (Jensen (1968; 1969)). Loosely speaking, Jensen's Alpha measures the difference of the actual excess return minus the expected excess return. Formally, the measure can be stated as

(43) $$Alpha_P = (R_P - R_0) - \beta_P \cdot (R_G - R_0)$$

$R_G - R_0$ is the excess return of a benchmark G over the risk-free rate. β_P is the sensitivity of the portfolio with respect to the factor G in a single index model. Hence, the second term on the right hand side of equation 43 measures the incorporated systematic risk times the excess return of the benchmark. The first term is the actual excess return of the portfolio. The difference between the two terms is called Jensen's Alpha and is often linked to the skills of a portfolio manager.

In order to generate Alpha, a portfolio manager has to deviate from the benchmark. However, a pension fund or other institutional investor might want to keep the deviations low. The Tracking Error is a measure to quantify these deviations.

(44) $$TE = \sqrt{1 - R^2} \cdot \sigma_P$$

The above formula describes the calculation of the Tracking Error. The R-squared measure is from a regression of portfolio excess returns on benchmark excess returns. The standard deviation of the portfolio returns is denoted by σ_P.

Treynor and Black (1973) suggest dividing the Alpha by the Tracking Error. This yields the so-called Information Ratio or Appraisal Ratio.

$$(45) \qquad IR = \frac{Alpha_P}{\sqrt{1-R^2} \cdot \sigma_P}$$

The Information Ratio is high if a portfolio manager achieves a high Alpha while keeping the Tracking Error low. In other words, the Information Ratio accounts for deviations from the benchmark.

An interesting question is how a portfolio manager can generate Alpha. As noted before, one requirement is the deviation from the benchmark. However, a simple deviation does not necessarily lead to a positive Alpha. One possibility which might also be important with respect to the forecasting models under investigation is a possible difference between the portfolio advice of Modern Portfolio Theory and actual investment behaviour. There might be risks, such as the previously mentioned cyclical risks, which are not captured by Modern Portfolio Theory. People fear bearing such risks. If these risks affect the average investor, there will be risk premia (Cochrane (1999a)). A portfolio manager who identifies such risks can generate Alpha by bearing such risks. However, these risks do not necessarily show up as volatility or covariance to the market portfolio. Hence, Beta might be low, and thus, the benchmark return times Beta is also low. At the same time, the average portfolio return could be high because of earning additional risk premia. I refer the interested reader to Spremann (2006, p. 385-388) for a detailed discussion with a focus on portfolio management.

With respect to performance measurement, the idea of Jensen's Alpha can be refined by applying a multifactor model. A multifactor model is able to detect additional sources of risk, which enables the determination of a more accurate Alpha. Therefore, the subsequent performance evaluations will include a multifactor approach based on the Fama-French Model.

(46) $$P_{k,t} = a_k + b_k \cdot MKT_t + c_k \cdot SMB_t + d_k \cdot HML_t + \varepsilon$$

Running regressions of the portfolio excess returns on MKT_t, SMB_t, and HML_t yields the three different exposures b_k, c_k, and d_k. These exposures quantify the incurred risks of an investment strategy with respect to MKT_t, SMB_t, and HML_t. It is yet not entirely clear which risks are covered by SMB_t, and HML_t. However, the discussion provided in the literature review and in Chapter 3 points at a link to changing business conditions, i.e., the real economy.

7.5. Style Rotation Strategies – 4 Style Portfolios

7.5.1. Fixed Predictor Portfolios

I start by setting up three simple strategies which will be developed to more complex strategies later. The starting point is an investor who has an investment opportunity set (IOS) of the four style portfolios SMALL, BIG, VALUE, and GROWTH. Additionally, some strategies are allowed to invest in a fixed income instrument at the 1-month LIBOR rate. After the calibration period, the next month's returns are forecasted for each of the portfolios in the IOS. The investor allocates his funds to the portfolio with the highest predicted return. The following table summarises some elements of the investment strategies.

Strategy	IOS	Calibration Method	Calibration Window	Investment Period
1a	SMALL, BIG, VALUE, GROWTH	Once	60 months	Jul1998-Jun2008
1b	SMALL, BIG, VALUE, GROWTH, LIBOR	Once	60 months	Jul1998-Jun2008
2a	SMALL, BIG, VALUE, GROWTH	Rolling	60 months	Jul1998-Jun2008
2b	SMALL, BIG, VALUE, GROWTH, LIBOR	Rolling	60 months	Jul1998-Jun2008
3a	SMALL, BIG, VALUE, GROWTH	Recursive	60 months*	Jul1998-Jun2008
3b	SMALL, BIG, VALUE, GROWTH, LIBOR	Recursive	60 months*	Jul1998-Jun2008

Table 27: Investment strategies with fixed predictor variables – 4 style portfolios
Table 27 exhibits some key characteristics of the investment strategies which apply a fixed predictor portfolio. There are three times two strategies which differ with respect to the calibration method. For each strategy, there is an alternative with a possible fixed income investment. The calibration period for the recursive window refers to the initial estimation period. Then, the window increases, which is indicated by *.

The above table exhibits some characteristics of the first three times two investment strategies. Each investment strategy is configured for two (sub) investment opportunity sets. One IOS is restricted to the four styles SMALL, BIG, VALUE, and GROWTH, while the other IOS contains an additional fixed income instrument which pays a return at the LIBOR rate. All strategies denoted by an "a" imply the restricted IOS. All strategies denoted by "b" allow investments in the fixed income instrument. The investor will allocate his funds to the fixed income instrument when he predicts negative excess returns for the four style portfolios. The forecasting models of strategies 1a and 1b are calibrated once with the data from Jul1993 to Jun1998, containing the returns of 60 months. The returns starting at Jul1998 are forecasted on this initial calibration. However, the models are updated every month with the last month's returns of the predictor portfolios in order to forecast the next month's returns of the four style portfolios SMALL, BIG, VALUE, and GROWTH. As can be seen from Table 17 the predictor portfolio is BH for all four styles. Recall that the predictor portfolio is the one which exhibits the highest serial or cross-serial correlation with the portfolio which will be forecasted. The explicit forecasting models applied in the strategies 1a and 1b are given in (47)

$$(47)\quad \begin{aligned} &SMALL\_RF_t = \alpha_S + \phi_S BH\_RF_{t-1} + \varepsilon_t \\ &BIG\_RF_t = \alpha_B + \phi_B BH\_RF_{t-1} + \varepsilon_t \\ &VALUE\_RF_t = \alpha_V + \phi_V BH\_RF_{t-1} + \varepsilon_t \\ &GROWTH\_RF_t = \alpha_G + \phi_G BH\_RF_{t-1} + \varepsilon_t \end{aligned}$$

After calibrating and forecasting the next month's return by (47), the funds are entirely allocated to the portfolio which has the highest forecasted return. The forecasting and investing steps are repeated from Jul1998 to May2008. Jun2008 is the last month for which a return is calculated. However, calibrating the model only once has a major drawback which is especially important when the predictor portfolio is the same in all forecasting models. If α is high in one of the forecasting models this model prefers the respective portfolio every time when a last month's return is low. A similar explanation holds for a model with a high value of ϕ. A portfolio which is forecasted by a model which has a high ϕ will be preferred if the last month's return of the predictor portfolio was high. Hence, other calibration approaches might be more appealing.

The investment strategies 2a, 2b, 3a, and 3b apply other approaches with respect to the calibration of the forecasting models. In 2a and 2b the parameters α and ϕ are estimated each month by applying a rolling window of 60 months. In 3a and 3b the parameters α and ϕ are estimated each month by applying a recursive window starting with 60 observations. Such calibration methods might be an improvement compared to the one-time-only calibration. Additional improvements can be implemented as time passes and new information becomes available. For example, the investor might realise that another predictor portfolio might have better forecasting power. Such an alternative is presented in section 7.5.2. However, before accounting for information from other points in time, the performance of the above investment strategies will be evaluated.

Strategy	# Transactions	Total Return	Mean (annualised)	Risk (annualised)
		Panel A: Investment period Jul1998-Jun2008		
1a	57	143.8%	8.9%	17.8%
1b	75	238.3%	12.2%	15.6%
2a	49	218.9%	11.6%	17.0%
2b	62	294.4%	13.7%	14.9%
3a	55	144.2%	8.9%	16.7%
3b	66	285.6%	13.5%	14.4%
MKT	-	17.5%	1.6%	15.0%
MIX	-	130.5%	8.4%	15.8%
		Panel B: Investment period Jul1998-Jun2003		
1a	25	-4.7%	-1.0%	20.9%
1b	35	20.1%	3.7%	17.9%
2a	25	-4.6%	-0.9%	18.4%
2b	32	23.3%	4.2%	15.1%
3a	23	-23.2%	-5.3%	18.1%
3b	30	17.7%	3.3%	15.2%
MKT	-	-30.3%	-7.2%	17.6%
MIX	-	-12.8%	-2.7%	18.0%
		Panel C: Investment period Jul2003-Jun2008		
1a	32	155.7%	18.8%	13.7%
1b	40	181.7%	20.7%	12.6%
2a	24	234.2%	24.1%	14.6%
2b	30	220.0%	23.3%	14.3%
3a	32	218.0%	23.1%	14.1%
3b	36	227.7%	23.7%	13.0%
MKT	-	68.4%	10.4%	11.6%
MIX	-	164.3%	19.4%	12.5%

Table 28: Risk and return of investment strategies with fixed predictor variables – 4 style portfolios
The above table presents basic evaluations of the previously described investment strategies and the market as well as MIX. Panel A covers the investment period Jul1998 to Jun2008. Panel B shows the evaluations for the subsample period Jul1998 to Jun2003 and Panel C provides the results for the subsample period Jul2003 to Jun2008. The number of transactions represents the number of switches between the four styles. Total returns are calculated with gross returns. The annual mean return and the standard deviation (Risk) are based on log returns.

Table 28 compares the three times two investment strategies to the market and a new benchmark portfolio called MIX. MIX is a portfolio whose investments are equally weighted in all the four styles SMALL, BIG, VALUE, and GROWTH. Such a portfolio is necessary in order to differentiate more clearly between forecasting effects and effects which are related to the portfolio construction. For example, MKT is a value-weighted index, and therefore, the weight attributed to small caps is low. In contrast, MIX invests the same amount in small caps as in large caps. This makes a substantial difference, as we can see from the above table. Nonetheless, over the entire investment period the active investment strategies clearly outperform MKT as well as MIX in terms of return. In addition, the risk, measured by the standard deviation of log returns, is not considerably different between the investment strategies and the market. However, the active investment strategies require frequent trading, as the number of transactions shows. The active investment strategies require at least 49 portfolio switches. Moreover, extending the IOS by a fixed income instrument causes even more frequent trading. Nevertheless, the strategies which allow for a fixed income investment have a higher total return and a lower risk than their counterparts without a fixed income instrument. The highest total return of all a-strategies is achieved by 2a, which is based on a rolling calibration window of 60 months. The highest total return of all b-strategies is achieved by strategy 2b, which is also based on a rolling window approach. Moreover, strategies 2a and 2b have a lower risk than their counterparts 1a and 1b. This might suggest that a calibration window which has more weight on the more recent past delivers superior results compared to the other calibration approaches.

The subsample periods show an interesting pattern. During the first part of the investment period, Jul1998 to Jun2003, all a-strategies have negative returns, while the b-strategies, those which allow fixed income investments, have positive returns. In other words, forecasting a negative return and acting upon this forecast by investing in a fixed income instrument seems to be profitable. Moreover, all a-strategies have higher returns than MKT and two of the three a-strategies also beat the benchmark portfolio MIX. The second part of the investment period, Jul2003 to Jun2008, shows positive returns of MKT, MIX, and all active investment strategies. All active investment strategies except 1a beat the benchmark portfolio MIX with respect to total return. The risk figures seem comparable among all portfolios in the first as well as in the second part of the investment period. However, a passive investment from Jul1998 to Jun2008 in SMALL yields a total return of 221.6%. Interestingly, all b-strategies exceed this result while the a-strategies remain below it.[15]

[15] The charts provided in the appendix focus on the comparison between the active strategies and an investment in SMALL.

Strategy	SMALL	BIG	VALUE	GROWTH	LIBOR
Panel A: Investment period Jul1998-Jun2008					
1a	11	81	0	28	0
1b	11	59	0	28	22
2a	24	9	65	22	0
2b	24	8	47	19	22
3a	27	6	58	29	0
3b	27	3	39	25	26
Panel B: Investment period Jul1998-Jun2003					
1a	4	42	0	14	0
1b	4	29	0	14	13
2a	4	7	27	22	0
2b	4	7	14	19	16
3a	8	4	19	29	0
3b	8	3	7	25	17
Panel C: Investment period Jul2003-Jun2008					
1a	7	39	0	14	0
1b	7	30	0	14	9
2a	20	2	38	0	0
2b	20	1	33	0	6
3a	19	2	39	0	0
3b	19	0	32	0	9

Table 29: Allocation of funds during investment period – fixed predictor variables and 4 style portfolios
Table 29 presents the number of months in which each strategy was invested in a particular style portfolio. Panel A covers the investment period Jul1998 to Jun2008. Panel B shows the evaluations for the subsample period Jul1998 to Jun2003 and Panel C displays the results for the subsample period Jul2003 to Jun2008. For example, over the entire investment period Strategy 1b was invested 11 months in small caps (SMALL), 59 months in large caps (BIG), 28 months in growth stocks (GROWTH), and 22 months in the fixed income instrument (LIBOR).

Table 29 sheds more light on the effect of different calibration methods. The table shows the number of months in which funds were allocated to a certain style for each of the three times two strategies. With Panel A in view strategies 1a and 1b, which are based on a single calibration period, switch primarily between large caps and growth stocks. However, introducing a fixed income instrument shifts some months from large caps to LIBOR, i.e., to the investments in the fixed income instrument. Intuitively, this seems appealing. An investor who predicts a negative return might invest in large caps as long as he is restricted to long positions in stocks. The strategies which are based on a rolling or recursive window approach show a quite different picture. As the parameters change over time, the funds are allocated more frequently to small caps and value stocks. Similar results hold for the two subperiods.

Strategy	Jensen's Alpha	CAPM Beta	Sharpe Ratio	Treynor Ratio	Tracking Error	Information Ratio
			Panel A: Investment period Jul1998-Jun2008			
1a	7.3%	1.09	0.41	0.07	7.2%	1.01
1b	10.6%	0.85	0.68	0.13	9.2%	1.15
2a	10.0%	0.89	0.59	0.11	10.5%	0.95
2b	12.1%	0.69	0.81	0.18	11.7%	1.03
3a	7.3%	0.87	0.44	0.08	10.5%	0.70
3b	11.9%	0.66	0.83	0.18	11.7%	1.01
MIX	6.8%	0.91	0.43	0.08	8.0%	0.85
			Panel B: Investment period Jul1998-Jun2003			
1a	7.0%	1.09	-0.13	-0.03	8.6%	0.82
1b	9.3%	0.83	0.10	0.02	10.9%	0.85
2a	4.7%	0.82	-0.15	-0.03	11.9%	0.40
2b	7.3%	0.54	0.16	0.04	14.2%	0.51
3a	0.1%	0.80	-0.39	-0.09	11.9%	0.01
3b	6.5%	0.56	0.09	0.03	13.9%	0.47
MIX	3.4%	0.88	-0.25	-0.05	9.3%	0.37
			Panel C: Investment period Jul2003-Jun2008			
1a	7.6%	1.08	1.27	0.16	5.6%	1.35
1b	11.3%	0.89	1.53	0.22	7.3%	1.55
2a	13.7%	1.00	1.55	0.23	8.9%	1.54
2b	13.1%	0.97	1.53	0.23	8.7%	1.50
3a	13.1%	0.96	1.54	0.23	8.6%	1.52
3b	15.0%	0.81	1.72	0.28	9.3%	1.62
MIX	9.7%	0.93	1.44	0.20	6.4%	1.51

Table 30: Performance measurement of investment strategies with fixed predictor variables – 4 style portfolios

Table 30 presents additional performance measures. Panel A covers the investment period Jul1998 to Jun2008. Panel B shows the evaluations for the subsample period Jul1998 to Jun2003 and Panel C presents the results for the subsample period Jul2003 to Jun2008. The calculations are based on monthly log excess returns covering the time period Jul1998 to Jun2008. The numbers are annualised wherever applicable. Calculations are conducted with reference to MKT where a benchmark is required.

Table 30 displays some of the performance measures introduced in section 7.4. Over the entire investment period the highest Sharpe Ratios within an IOS-group can be found for strategies 2a and 3b, respectively. Hence, these two strategies have the highest reward per unit of risk. Regression analyses also reveal the highest Alpha for these two strategies. In contrast, the Betas are not higher than those of the other strategies. This is also apparent in the high Treynor Ratios of 2a and 3b. However, the Tracking Error is also high for 2a and 3b, which means large deviations from the market portfolio MKT. The high deviations have a lowering impact on the Information Ratio. Similar conclusions hold for the two subsample periods. However, as outlined in section 7.4., the variation of returns might be an insufficient measure of risk as some risks might not be captured by Modern Portfolio Theory. In order to obtain a more comprehensive picture of the risks associated with the investment strategies, a multi factor model is applied.

Strategy	FF Alpha	Market Beta	Size Beta	Value Beta
Panel A: Investment period Jul1998-Jun2008				
1a	5.1% *	1.19 *	0.23 *	0.16 *
1b	8.3% *	0.96 *	0.21 *	0.23 *
2a	2.9%	1.20 *	0.74 *	0.48 *
2b	6.5% *	0.94 *	0.59 *	0.40 *
3a	1.4%	1.13 *	0.63 *	0.38 *
3b	6.8% *	0.89 *	0.51 *	0.42 *
MIX	3.3%	1.11 *	0.57 *	0.24 *
Panel B: Investment period Jul1998-Jun2003				
1a	6.8%	1.21 *	0.28 *	0.10
1b	8.9%	0.98 *	0.30 *	0.16
2a	3.4%	1.24 *	0.78 *	0.46 *
2b	6.6%	0.77 *	0.41 *	0.25
3a	-0.3%	1.06 *	0.60 *	0.18
3b	5.9%	0.80 *	0.46 *	0.23
MIX	3.0%	1.15 *	0.62 *	0.18 *
Panel C: Investment period Jul2003-Jun2008				
1a	5.0% *	1.12 *	0.19 *	0.33 *
1b	10.0% *	0.91 *	0.10	0.40 *
2a	3.8%	1.13 *	0.71 *	0.59 *
2b	2.7%	1.11 *	0.75 *	0.49 *
3a	4.5%	1.08 *	0.62 *	0.72 *
3b	7.9% *	0.91 *	0.52 *	0.72 *
MIX	1.9%	1.03 *	0.56 *	0.41 *

Table 31: Three-factor evaluation of investment strategies with fixed predictor variables – 4 style portfolios
Table 31 shows the results of a time series regression analysis with MKT and the two long-short portfolios SMB and HML as explanatory variables. Panel A covers the investment period Jul1998 to Jun2008. Panel B shows the evaluations for the subsample period Jul1998 to Jun2003 and Panel C displays the results for the subsample period Jul2003 to Jun2008.

$$P_{k,t} = a_k + b_k \cdot MKT_t + c_k \cdot SMB_t + d_k \cdot HML_t + \varepsilon$$

The monthly excess return $P_{k,t}$ of a portfolio k at t is regressed on the three factors MKT_t, SMB_t, and HML_t. The market beta is referred to as b_k, the size beta as c_k and the value beta as d_k. The constant, which is referred to as Fama-French Alpha (FF Alpha), is represented by a_k and shown as an annualised number. An asterisk indicates significance at the 5% level.

The above table exhibits the results from a regression approach which makes use of the Fama-French Factors. Referring to Panel A, we can see that all strategies have positive exposures to the three factors. The market beta is around one for all strategies. In contrast, the size and value betas strongly differ among the strategies. More precisely, Strategy 2a exhibits the highest exposure to all factors while strategies 1a and 1b show more moderate exposures to SMB and HML. In other words, Strategy 2a has high returns in months in which small caps or value stocks have high returns. Moreover, the exposures to the risk factors SMB and HML are significant across the various investment strategies. Hence, it can be concluded that the high returns of the above described style rotation strategies are partly attributable to additional risks not captured by the CAPM. However, even after accounting for the Fama-French Factors there remains a considerable Alpha. Interestingly, the Alpha is higher for the strategies 1a and 1b than for the rolling window based strategies 2a and 2b. The extension of the IOS by a fixed income instrument results in a higher Alpha for all strategies. The results for the subperiods are somewhat different. Although the magnitude of the Alphas is high, there is no more significance at the 5% level in the first half of the investment period. However, the loss of significance may also be attributable to the lower number of observations.

The above analyses suggest an outperformance of the active investment strategy compared to MKT and MIX. Moreover, with the predominance of the investment strategies over MIX in view, there seems to be a clear advantage in applying forecasting models. In other words, the forecasting based rotation among the four style portfolios and LIBOR delivers superior results compared to a buy and hold portfolio which attributes equal weights to the four strategies. However, it might be of interest to have further information on the sources of the outperformance.

Strategy	MKT_RF < 0	MKT_RF > 0	MIX_RF < 0	MIX_RF > 0
Investment period: Jul1998-Jun2008				
1a	-3.9%	3.7%	-4.3%	3.6%
1b	-2.7%	3.4%	-3.0%	3.2%
2a	-2.9%	3.4%	-4.0%	3.7%
2b	-2.0%	3.1%	-2.8%	3.3%
3a	-3.1%	3.2%	-4.1%	3.5%
3b	-2.0%	3.0%	-2.6%	3.1%
MKT	-4.0%	2.8%	-3.8%	2.3%
MIX	-3.1%	3.1%	-4.0%	3.3%

Table 32: Conditional mean excess returns of investment strategies with fixed predictor variables – 4 style portfolios

Table 32 presents the mean log excess returns of the investment strategies under the condition that the log excess return of MKT or MIX is negative (MKT_RF < 0, MIX_RF < 0) or positive (MKT_RF > 0, MIX_RF > 0). The calculations are based on monthly data.

In order to gain additional insight, the conditional mean excess returns are calculated and shown in Table 32. Consider the column "MKT_RF < 0". The average negative monthly excess return of MKT is -4.0%. During the same months, Strategy 2a has a negative return of -2.9% and Strategy 2b performed on average by -2.0%. Based on the same months, MIX achieved an average log excess return of -3.1% per month. Now consider the values in the column "MKT_RF > 0". Taking the averages of the months in which the market had a positive return reveals a positive average log excess return of 3.4% for Strategy 2a and a positive log excess return of 3.1% for Strategy 2b. The conditional value for MIX is 3.1%. The representations in Table 32 provide additional information about the performance of the active investment strategies. For example, Strategy2a exhibits a less negative value than MIX or MKT under the condition that MKT is negative. Hence, either the excess returns of 2a are frequently higher (less negative or positive) than those of MKT and MIX or there must be huge positive returns which compensate for strongly negative returns of 2a. In other words, either the funds are frequently allocated to an outperforming portfolio or the funds are allocated to portfolios which then have sometimes very high returns. Of course, there is the possibility of a combination of both. Moreover, the differences between the investment strategies and MIX are much lower than the differences between the strategies and MKT. This confirms the above evidence that a part of the outperformance is attributable to the portfolio construction procedure. However, the b-strategies show a considerable difference to MIX, conditional on negative market excess returns. This indicates an effect of the IOS. Similar but less clear conclusions hold when MIX is used as the conditional portfolio. This is shown in the two right hand side columns of Table 32 and is further investigated below.

Strategy	Minus Months	Conditional MMs	Detected
	Investment period: Jul1998-Jun2008		
1a	41	38	
1b	29	26	19
2a	46	41	
2b	30	27	18
3a	48	43	
3b	29	26	19
MIX	45	45	

Table 33: Unconditional and conditional number of negative log excess returns of investment strategies with fixed predictor variables – 4 style portfolios
Table 33 presents the number of monthly negative log excess returns for each of the strategies which are based on fixed predictor variables as well as for the benchmark MIX. The number of unconditional negative excess returns is listed in the column Minus Months. The number of conditional negative excess returns is shown in the column Conditional MMs. The condition is a negative excess return of MIX in the respective month. The number of correctly predicted negative returns is shown in the column Detected.

Table 33 sheds further light on the forecasting power of the models. Over the entire investment period of Jul1998 to Jun2008, MIX exhibits 45 months with a negative log excess return. Overall, the active investment strategies had between 29 and 48 months with negative log excess returns. With respect to avoiding negative excess returns, the b-strategies might be of more interest than the a-strategies, which do not allow fixed income investments. Consider, for example, strategy 2b and the benchmark portfolio MIX in the above table. MIX had 45 months with negative excess returns. By following the investment strategy 2b, the same months were negative in 27 cases. Hence, there are 18 months which were correctly predicted as negative, and a long position in the fixed income instrument or in a portfolio with a positive excess return was taken. However, there are also 3 months which had a positive MIX return but Strategy 2b had a negative return.

7.5.2. Changing Predictor Portfolios

The models presented in section 7.5.1. are based on the assumption that the predictor portfolios are determined at Jun1998 and then applied throughout the investment period. An alternative approach would be to check at some intervals whether other portfolios might have a superior forecasting power. This is the topic of the current section.

In order to identify predictor portfolios, I again rely on the estimated lead-lag relationships from section 6.1. As shown above, the lead-lag relationships change over time. For example, we could observe a shift towards growth stocks in the second subsample period. Hence, it may be a promising approach to substitute BH_RF in the above forecasting models with a growth portfolio in Jun2003. However, the length of the interval after which an investor checks for superior predictors can be chosen arbitrarily. In order to keep the analyses consistent, I chose an interval of 60 months, which equals the length of the subsample periods. Therefore, the procedure is enriched with an additional task. As in the previous section, the investment period starts with Jul1998. The returns of the period Jul1998 to Jun2003 are forecasted with the same models as above and a long position in the portfolio with the highest forecasted return is taken. In Jun2003 the investor tests for superior forecasting power of other portfolios. In other words, in Jun2003 the lead-lag relationships of the past 60 months are considered. Then, for each style the portfolio with the highest (cross-)serial correlation coefficient is chosen as the predictor portfolio.

$$\begin{aligned} &SMALL\_RF_t = \alpha_S + \phi_S BH\_RF_{t-1} + \varepsilon_t \\ &BIG\_RF_t = \alpha_B + \phi_B BH\_RF_{t-1} + \varepsilon_t \\ &VALUE\_RF_t = \alpha_V + \phi_V BH\_RF_{t-1} + \varepsilon_t \\ &GROWTH\_RF_t = \alpha_G + \phi_G BH\_RF_{t-1} + \varepsilon_t \end{aligned} \tag{48}$$

(48) shows the models which have Jul1993 to Jun1998 as initial estimation period. These are the same models as in the previous section. However, in Jun2003 the investor checks for better models with data of the past 60 months.

$$\begin{aligned} &SMALL\_RF_t = \alpha_S + \phi_S GROWTH\_RF_{t-1} + \varepsilon_t \\ &BIG\_RF_t = \alpha_B + \phi_B BL\_RF_{t-1} + \varepsilon_t \\ &VALUE\_RF_t = \alpha_V + \phi_V BL\_RF_{t-1} + \varepsilon_t \\ &GROWTH\_RF_t = \alpha_G + \phi_G GROWTH\_RF_{t-1} + \varepsilon_t \end{aligned} \tag{49}$$

As Table 18 shows, the lead-lag relationships have changed compared to those of the first subsample period. Thus, the predictor variables are adjusted, as shown in (49).

This means that the returns for Jul1998 to Jun2003 are forecasted by (48) and the returns for Jul2003 to Jun2008 are forecasted by the models represented in (49). However, the model parameters are subject to the same calibration procedures as above.

Strategy	IOS	Calibration Method	Calibration Window	Investment Period
4a	SMALL, BIG, VALUE, GROWTH	Once with change	60 months	Jul1998-Jun2008
4b	SMALL, BIG, VALUE, GROWTH, LIBOR	Once with change	60 months	Jul1998-Jun2008
5a	SMALL, BIG, VALUE, GROWTH	Rolling with change	60 months	Jul1998-Jun2008
5b	SMALL, BIG, VALUE, GROWTH, LIBOR	Rolling with change	60 months	Jul1998-Jun2008
6a	SMALL, BIG, VALUE, GROWTH	Recursive with change	60 months*	Jul1998-Jun2008
6b	SMALL, BIG, VALUE, GROWTH, LIBOR	Recursive with change	60 months*	Jul1998-Jun2008

Table 34: Investment strategies with changing predictor variables – 4 style portfolios
Table 34 presents some key characteristics of the investment strategies which apply a changing predictor portfolio. There are three times two strategies which differ with respect to the calibration method. For each strategy, there is an alternative with a possible fixed income investment. The calibration period for the recursive window refers to the initial estimation period. Then, the window increases, which is indicated by *.

Table 34 is analogue to Table 27 and presents some basic characteristics of the strategies. The evaluations of the investment strategies with changing predictor variables are analogue to those of the strategies with fixed predictor variables. There are again three times two investment strategies which differ with respect to the IOS. The sole difference to the previously evaluated investment strategies lies in the predictor variables which are adjusted after the first 60 months of the investment period. Moreover, I take the previously developed investment strategies as reference units for the subsequent investment strategies. More precisely, I compare strategy 4a to 1a, 4b to 1b, 5a to 2a, 5b to 2b, 6a to 3a, and 6b to 3b. This is an appealing comparison as it answers the question whether an adjustment of the predictor portfolios improves the performance of the strategies or not.

Strategy	# Transactions	Total Return	Mean (annualised)	Risk (annualised)
Panel A: Investment period Jul1998-Jun2008				
4a	53	199.7%	11.0%	18.1%
4b	71	189.8%	10.6%	16.1%
5a	48	198.8%	10.9%	16.7%
5b	60	255.0%	12.7%	14.8%
6a	52	130.3%	8.3%	16.6%
6b	66	188.5%	10.6%	14.7%
MKT	-	17.5%	1.6%	15.0%
MIX	-	130.5%	8.4%	15.8%
Panel B: Investment period Jul1998-Jun2003				
4a	25	-4.7%	-1.0%	20.9%
4b	35	20.1%	3.7%	17.9%
5a	25	-4.6%	-0.9%	18.4%
5b	32	23.3%	4.2%	15.1%
6a	23	-23.2%	-5.3%	18.1%
6b	30	17.7%	3.3%	15.2%
MKT	-	-30.3%	-7.2%	17.6%
MIX	-	-12.8%	-2.7%	18.0%
Panel C: Investment period Jul2003-Jun2008				
4a	28	214.4%	22.9%	14.2%
4b	36	141.3%	17.6%	14.0%
5a	23	213.1%	22.8%	14.1%
5b	28	188.0%	21.2%	14.1%
6a	29	199.9%	22.0%	14.0%
6b	36	145.2%	17.9%	13.9%
MKT	-	68.4%	10.4%	11.6%
MIX	-	164.3%	19.4%	12.5%

Table 35: Risk and return of investment strategies with changing predictor variables – 4 style portfolios
The above table presents basic evaluations of the previously described investment strategies and the market as well as MIX. Panel A covers the investment period Jul1998 to Jun2008. Panel B shows the evaluations for the subsample period Jul1998 to Jun2003 and Panel C displays the results for the subsample period Jul2003 to Jun2008. The number of transactions represents the number of switches between the four styles. Total returns are calculated with gross returns. The annual mean return and the standard deviation (Risk) are based on log returns.

The introduction of changing predictor variables lowers the number of transactions, as we can see by comparing Table 35 to Table 28. For example, strategy 4a requires 53 transactions, while the corresponding strategy with fixed predictor variables, namely 1a, requires 57 transactions. Similar differences hold for the other strategies. Moreover, changing the forecasting variables in Jun2003 also affects the risk and return measures. Overall, the total returns are considerably lower when the forecasting variables are changed. However, changing the forecasting variables improves the total return of 4a as it has a higher total return than 1a. The comparison of the subperiods can be restricted to the window Jul2003 to Jun2008 as the first part of the investment period is identical to the previous section. Generally, changing the predictor variables lowers the total return of the investment strategies. In other words, the strategies which are based on adjusted predictor variables have lower returns than their counterparts of the previous section which apply the same predictor portfolios throughout the investment period.

Strategy	SMALL	BIG	VALUE	GROWTH	LIBOR
		Panel A: Investment period Jul1998-Jun2008			
4a	36	42	28	14	0
4b	35	29	19	14	23
5a	34	7	56	23	0
5b	33	7	40	19	21
6a	42	4	45	29	0
6b	40	3	26	25	26
		Panel B: Investment period Jul1998-Jun2003			
4a	4	42	0	14	0
4b	4	29	0	14	13
5a	4	7	27	22	0
5b	4	7	14	19	16
6a	8	4	19	29	0
6b	8	3	7	25	17
		Panel C: Investment period Jul2003-Jun2008			
4a	32	0	28	0	0
4b	31	0	19	0	10
5a	30	0	29	1	0
5b	29	0	26	0	5
6a	34	0	26	0	0
6b	32	0	19	0	9

Table 36: Allocation of funds during investment period – changing predictor variables and 4 style portfolios

Table 36 presents the number of months in which each strategy was invested in a particular style portfolio. Panel A covers the investment period Jul1998 to Jun2008. Panel B shows the evaluations for the subsample period Jul1998 to Jun2003 and Panel C presents the results for the subsample period Jul2003 to Jun2008. For example, over the entire investment period Strategy 4b was invested 35 months in small caps (SMALL), 29 months in large caps (BIG), 19 months in value stocks (VALUE), 14 months in growth stocks (GROWTH), and 23 months in the fixed income instrument (LIBOR).

As Panel A of Table 36 shows, strategies 4a and 4b allocate the funds frequently to other styles. Strategies which apply a rolling or recursive window approach in their forecasting models provide a more focused picture with infrequent investments in large caps. Compared to the previous strategies there seems to be a trend towards small caps. However, the allocations to the fixed income instrument are not substantially affected by changing forecasting variables. Note that the differences are solely attributable to the second part of the investment period.

Strategy	Jensen's Alpha	CAPM Beta	Sharpe Ratio	Treynor Ratio	Tracking Error	Information Ratio
			Panel A: Investment period Jul1998-Jun2008			
4a	9.4%	1.05	0.52	0.09	8.9%	1.05
4b	9.1%	0.84	0.56	0.11	10.4%	0.87
5a	9.4%	0.87	0.56	0.11	10.7%	0.88
5b	11.1%	0.67	0.75	0.17	12.0%	0.92
6a	6.7%	0.86	0.41	0.08	10.6%	0.63
6b	9.0%	0.67	0.61	0.14	11.8%	0.76
MIX	6.8%	0.91	0.43	0.08	8.0%	0.85
			Panel B: Investment period Jul1998-Jun2003			
4a	7.0%	1.09	-0.13	-0.03	8.6%	0.82
4b	9.3%	0.83	0.10	0.02	10.9%	0.85
5a	4.7%	0.82	-0.15	-0.03	11.9%	0.40
5b	7.3%	0.54	0.16	0.04	14.2%	0.51
6a	0.1%	0.80	-0.39	-0.09	11.9%	0.01
6b	6.5%	0.56	0.09	0.03	13.9%	0.47
MIX	3.4%	0.88	-0.25	-0.05	9.3%	0.37
			Panel C: Investment period Jul2003-Jun2008			
4a	13.2%	0.93	1.52	0.23	9.3%	1.41
4b	8.4%	0.87	1.16	0.19	9.9%	0.85
5a	13.1%	0.92	1.51	0.23	9.3%	1.41
5b	11.5%	0.91	1.40	0.22	9.4%	1.22
6a	12.3%	0.92	1.47	0.22	9.1%	1.35
6b	8.6%	0.89	1.19	0.19	9.5%	0.90
MIX	9.7%	0.93	1.44	0.20	6.4%	1.51

Table 37: Performance measurement of investment strategies with changing predictor variables – 4 style portfolios

Table 37 presents additional performance measures. Panel A covers the investment period Jul1998 to Jun2008. Panel B shows the evaluations for the subsample period Jul1998 to Jun2003 and Panel C presents the results for the subsample period Jul2003 to Jun2008. The calculations are based on monthly log excess returns covering the time period Jul1998 to Jun2008. The numbers are annualised wherever applicable. Calculations are conducted with reference to MKT, where a benchmark is required.

The numbers in Table 37 can be compared to those of Table 30 in order to see the effect of changing the predictor portfolios. Overall, changing the predictor variables in Jun2003 does not seem to alter the numbers substantially. The differences most worthy of mention can be found in Jensen's Alpha. For instance, Jensen's Alpha is considerably higher in Strategy 4a than in Strategy 1a. This increase can be attributed to the second part of the investment period. However, except for 4a, all strategies with changing predictor portfolios exhibit a lower Alpha than their counterparts with fixed predictors.

Strategy	FF Alpha	Market Beta	Size Beta	Value Beta
	Panel A: Investment period Jul1998-Jun2008			
4a	5.0% *	1.23 *	0.47 *	0.25 *
4b	4.5%	1.03 *	0.49 *	0.28 *
5a	2.0%	1.19 *	0.77 *	0.48 *
5b	5.2%	0.93 *	0.60 *	0.42 *
6a	0.4%	1.12 *	0.70 *	0.32 *
6b	3.2%	0.92 *	0.62 *	0.36 *
MIX	3.3%	1.11 *	0.57 *	0.24 *
	Panel B: Investment period Jul1998-Jun2003			
4a	6.8%	1.21 *	0.28 *	0.10
4b	8.9%	0.98 *	0.30 *	0.16
5a	3.4%	1.24 *	0.78 *	0.46 *
5b	6.6%	0.77 *	0.41 *	0.25
6a	-0.3%	1.06 *	0.60 *	0.18
6b	5.9%	0.80 *	0.46 *	0.23
MIX	3.0%	1.15 *	0.62 *	0.18 *
	Panel C: Investment period Jul2003-Jun2008			
4a	1.7%	1.08 *	0.83 *	0.61 *
4b	-3.2%	1.02 *	0.84 *	0.52 *
5a	1.7%	1.07 *	0.82 *	0.61 *
5b	0.1%	1.07 *	0.82 *	0.60 *
6a	0.7%	1.07 *	0.83 *	0.57 *
6b	-3.2%	1.04 *	0.84 *	0.50 *
MIX	1.9%	1.03 *	0.56 *	0.41 *

Table 38: Three-factor evaluation of investment strategies with changing variables – 4 style portfolios
Table 38 shows the results of a time series regression analysis with MKT and the two long-short portfolios SMB and HML as explanatory variables. Panel A covers the investment period Jul1998 to Jun2008. Panel B shows the evaluations for the subsample period Jul1998 to Jun2003 and Panel C displays the results for the subsample period Jul2003 to Jun2008.

$$P_{k,t} = a_k + b_k \cdot MKT_t + c_k \cdot SMB_t + d_k \cdot HML_t + \varepsilon$$

The monthly excess return $P_{k,t}$ of a portfolio k at t is regressed on the three factors MKT_t, SMB_t, and HML_t. The market beta is referred to as b_k, the size beta as c_k and the value beta as d_k. The constant which is referred to as Fama-French Alpha (FF Alpha) is represented by a_k and shown as an annualised number. An asterisk indicates significance at the 5% level.

Applying the Fama-French Model additionally lowers the magnitudes of the Alpha measures, which can be seen in Table 38. Moreover, introducing a fixed income instrument changes the order of the Alphas for strategies 4a and 4b compared to their fixed predictor counterparts 1a and 1b. The other strategies keep the order. However, the lower Alphas are accompanied by higher exposures to the risk factors. Hence, the returns of strategies 4a to 6b seem to be associated with higher risks than the returns of strategies 1a to 3b. Moreover, the magnitude of the Alphas seems considerably lower than in the previous section. This is accentuated by two negative Alphas. However, there is no significance at the 5% level.

Strategy	MKT_RF < 0	MKT_RF > 0	MIX_RF < 0	MIX_RF > 0
	Investment period: Jul1998-Jun2008			
4a	-3.4%	3.7%	-4.1%	3.7%
4b	-2.6%	3.1%	-3.2%	3.1%
5a	-2.8%	3.3%	-3.8%	3.5%
5b	-2.0%	3.0%	-2.7%	3.1%
6a	-3.0%	3.0%	-4.0%	3.3%
6b	-2.1%	2.8%	-2.8%	2.9%
MKT	-4.0%	2.8%	-3.8%	2.3%
MIX	-3.1%	3.1%	-4.0%	3.3%

Table 39: Conditional mean excess returns of investment strategies with changing predictor variables – 4 style portfolios
Table 39 presents the mean log excess returns of the investment strategies under the condition that the log excess return of MKT or MIX is negative (MKT_RF < 0, MIX_RF < 0) or positive (MKT_RF > 0, MIX_RF > 0). The calculations are based on monthly data.

Tables 39 and 40 provide the values of conditional evaluations. As before, the condition is either a negative log excess return of MKT or MIX. The values of Table 39 are almost identical to those of the previously shown fixed predictor strategies. The same is true for the number of negative and conditional negative months of Table 40.

Strategy	Minus Months	Conditional MMs	Detected
	Investment period: Jul1998-Jun2008		
4a	39	36	
4b	30	28	17
5a	43	38	
5b	29	26	19
6a	46	40	
6b	30	27	18
MIX	45	45	

Table 40: Unconditional and conditional number of negative log excess returns of investment strategies with changing predictor variables – 4 style portfolios
Table 40 presents the number of monthly negative log excess returns for each of the strategies which are based on changing predictor variables as well as for the benchmark MIX. The number of unconditional negative excess returns is listed in the column Minus Months. The number of conditional negative excess returns is shown in the column Conditional MMs. The condition is a negative excess return of MIX in the respective month. The number of correctly predicted negative returns is shown in the column Detected.

Generally speaking, the above evidence does not support an adjustment of the predictor variables after 60 months. However, the analysis is restricted to a one-time-only change at Jun2003. Therefore, it cannot be ruled out that other adjustment frequencies might exhibit superior results. Moreover, a more frequent adjustment of the predictor variables could be combined with another calibration period. However, in order to stay focused and keep the strategies clearly represented, I restrict the combinations to those evaluated above.

7.6. Style Rotation Strategies – 6 Style Portfolios

7.6.1. Fixed Predictor Portfolios

The present and subsequent section enrich the above-evaluated investment strategies with a finer partition of the investment opportunity set. The following strategies allow investments in all of the six Fama-French Portfolios SH, SM, SL, BH, BM, and BL. In addition, some strategies again allow an investment in a fixed income instrument at the LIBOR rate. However, the same calibration procedures and evaluations as above are performed. Thus, I will keep the explanations brief.

Strategy	IOS	Calibration Method	Calibration Window	Investment Period
1a_6	SH, SM, SL, BH, BM, BL	Once	60 months	Jul1998-Jun2008
1b_6	SH, SM, SL, BH, BM, BL, LIBOR	Once	60 months	Jul1998-Jun2008
2a_6	SH, SM, SL, BH, BM, BL	Rolling	60 months	Jul1998-Jun2008
2b_6	SH, SM, SL, BH, BM, BL, LIBOR	Rolling	60 months	Jul1998-Jun2008
3a_6	SH, SM, SL, BH, BM, BL	Recursive	60 months*	Jul1998-Jun2008
3b_6	SH, SM, SL, BH, BM, BL, LIBOR	Recursive	60 months*	Jul1998-Jun2008

Table 41: Investment strategies with fixed predictor variables – 6 style portfolios
Table 41 presents some key characteristics of the investment strategies which apply a fixed predictor portfolio. There are three times two strategies which differ with respect to the calibration method. For each strategy, there is an alternative with a possible fixed income investment. The calibration period for the recursive window refers to the initial estimation period. Then, the window increases, which is indicated by *.

The above table exhibits some characteristics of the first three times two investment strategies which apply finer partitioned market segments as IOS. As before, each investment strategy is evaluated for two versions of the IOS. One version is restricted to the six combined styles SH, SM, SL, BH, BM, and BL, while the other IOS contains an additional fixed income instrument which pays a return at the 1-month LIBOR rate. All strategies denoted by an "a" imply the restricted IOS. All strategies denoted by "b" allow fixed income investments. As above, the investor will allocate his funds to the fixed income instrument when he predicts negative excess returns for all of the six style portfolios. The forecasting models of strategies 1a_6 and 1b_6 are calibrated once with the data from Jul1993 to Jun1998, containing the returns of 60 months. The returns starting at Jul1998 are forecasted on this initial calibration. However, the models are updated every month with the last month's returns of the predictor portfolios in order to forecast the next month's returns of the six portfolios. As can be seen from Table 17, the predictor portfolio is BH for all six styles. Recall that the predictor portfolio is the one which exhibits the highest serial or cross-serial correlation with the portfolio which will be forecasted. The explicit forecasting models applied in the strategies 1a_6 and 1b_6 are given in (50)

$$
(50) \quad
\begin{aligned}
SH\_RF_t &= \alpha_{SH} + \phi_{SH} BH\_RF_{t-1} + \varepsilon_t \\
SM\_RF_t &= \alpha_{SM} + \phi_{SM} BH\_RF_{t-1} + \varepsilon_t \\
SL\_RF_t &= \alpha_{SL} + \phi_{SL} BH\_RF_{t-1} + \varepsilon_t \\
BH\_RF_t &= \alpha_{BH} + \phi_{BH} BH\_RF_{t-1} + \varepsilon_t \\
BM\_RF_t &= \alpha_{BM} + \phi_{BM} BH\_RF_{t-1} + \varepsilon_t \\
BL\_RF_t &= \alpha_{BL} + \phi_{BL} BH\_RF_{t-1} + \varepsilon_t
\end{aligned}
$$

After calibrating the models and forecasting the next month's returns by (50), the funds are entirely allocated to the portfolio which has the highest forecasted return. The forecasting and investing steps are repeated from Jul1998 to May2008. Jun2008 is the last month for which a return is calculated.

As outlined before, other calibration approaches are applied as well. In 2a_6 and 2b_6 the parameters α and ϕ are estimated each month by applying a rolling window of 60 months. In 3a_6 and 3b_6 the parameters α and ϕ are estimated each month by applying a recursive window starting with 60 observations.

Strategy	# Transactions	Total Return	Mean (annualised)	Risk (annualised)
Panel A: Investment period Jul1998-Jun2008				
1a_6	64	198.5%	10.9%	17.0%
1b_6	88	219.3%	11.6%	16.3%
2a_6	64	340.5%	14.8%	18.6%
2b_6	77	430.7%	16.7%	17.9%
3a_6	75	413.5%	16.4%	17.8%
3b_6	83	456.2%	17.2%	16.9%
MKT	-	17.5%	1.6%	15.0%
MIX6	-	117.1%	7.8%	16.2%
Panel B: Investment period Jul1998-Jun2003				
1a_6	29	18.0%	3.3%	18.0%
1b_6	42	22.0%	4.0%	16.8%
2a_6	29	41.9%	7.0%	19.1%
2b_6	38	75.3%	11.2%	18.0%
3a_6	33	42.7%	7.1%	19.1%
3b_6	37	53.6%	8.6%	17.8%
MKT	-	-30.3%	-7.2%	17.6%
MIX6	-	-16.7%	-3.6%	18.7%
Panel C: Investment period Jul2003-Jun2008				
1a_6	35	153.1%	18.6%	15.8%
1b_6	46	161.8%	19.2%	15.5%
2a_6	35	210.5%	22.7%	17.9%
2b_6	39	202.8%	22.2%	17.8%
3a_6	42	259.9%	25.6%	16.1%
3b_6	46	262.2%	25.7%	15.7%
MKT	-	68.4%	10.4%	11.6%
MIX6	-	160.6%	19.2%	12.6%

Table 42: Risk and return of investment strategies with fixed predictor variables – 6 style portfolios
The above table presents basic evaluations of the previously described investment strategies and the market as well as MIX6. Panel A covers the investment period Jul1998 to Jun2008. Panel B shows the evaluations for the subsample period Jul1998 to Jun2003 and Panel C displays the results for the subsample period Jul2003 to Jun2008. The number of transactions represents the number of switches between the four styles. Total returns are calculated with gross returns. The annual mean return and the standard deviation (Risk) are based on log returns.

The values in Panel A of Table 42 allow a first comparison of the strategies. With respect to total return, all active investment strategies outperform MKT. Moreover, the strategies also beat a new benchmark portfolio called MIX6. MIX6 is an equally weighted portfolio which covers all six Fama-French Portfolios. In other words, MIX6 invests 1/6 in each of the portfolios SH, SM, SL, BH, BM, and BL. With respect to risk, we can see that all strategies exhibit a slightly higher standard deviation than MKT or MIX6. However, the considerable outperformance does not seem to be adequately linked to conventional risk measures. The strategies can also be compared to their counterparts with an IOS of four style portfolios. Such a comparison reveals more transactions, a higher total return in 5 of the 6 strategies, and almost the same risk. However, one might wonder whether a passive investment in the best performing combined style yields a superior result. This is not the case. The highest total return, which amounts to 282%, can be observed for the SH portfolio. Hence, 4 of the 6 active investment strategies presented beat this portfolio with respect to total return.[16]

Panel B provides the values of the investment period Jul1998 to Jun2003. In contrast to MKT and MIX6, all active investment strategies have a positive total return. Interestingly, this is not the case for the earlier evaluated strategies with four style portfolios as IOS. In other words, the finer partition of the IOS causes some strategies to become positive. With respect to the second half of the investment period, we can see that the total return figures are of about the same magnitude as with four style portfolios as IOS. Hence, the higher total returns of the investment strategies 1a_6 to 3b_6 compared to their counterparts 1a to 3b are mostly attributable to the first half of the investment period when the aggregate market had a negative total return.

[16] The charts provided in the appendix compare the cumulative returns of each active strategy to a buy and hold investment in SH.

Strategy	SH	SM	SL	BH	BM	BL	LIBOR
Panel A: Investment period Jul1998-Jun2008							
1a_6	0	0	18	25	0	77	0
1b_6	0	0	18	25	0	61	16
2a_6	40	4	39	21	2	14	0
2b_6	28	4	39	21	0	12	16
3a_6	38	4	45	9	0	24	0
3b_6	30	4	45	9	0	14	18
Panel B: Investment period Jul1998-Jun2003							
1a_6	0	0	8	11	0	41	0
1b_6	0	0	8	11	0	32	9
2a_6	17	3	16	11	0	13	0
2b_6	8	3	16	11	0	11	11
3a_6	13	4	21	2	0	20	0
3b_6	8	4	21	2	0	14	11
Panel C: Investment period Jul2003-Jun2008							
1a_6	0	0	10	14	0	36	0
1b_6	0	0	10	14	0	29	7
2a_6	23	1	23	10	2	1	0
2b_6	20	1	23	10	0	1	5
3a_6	25	0	24	7	0	4	0
3b_6	22	0	24	7	0	0	7

Table 43: Allocation of funds during investment period – fixed predictor variables and 6 style portfolios
Table 43 presents the number of months in which each strategy was invested in a particular style portfolio. Panel A covers the investment period Jul1998 to Jun2008. Panel B shows the evaluations for the subsample period Jul1998 to Jun2003 and Panel C presents the results for the subsample period Jul2003 to Jun2008. For example, over the entire investment period strategy 2b_6 was invested 28 months in small value stocks (SH), 4 months in small neutral stocks (SM), 39 months in small growth stocks (SL), 21 months in large value stocks (BH), 12 months in large growth stocks (BL), and 16 months in the fixed income instrument (LIBOR).

The higher number of transactions seems to be in line with a larger IOS. Table 43 shows the number of months that each strategy was invested in a particular portfolio. Interestingly, the finer partition of the IOS causes a fund allocation to more extreme portfolios such as small value or small growth. The two portfolios SM and BM are only used a few times. These findings hold for the entire investment period as well as for the two subperiods.

Strategy	Jensen's Alpha	CAPM Beta	Sharpe Ratio	Treynor Ratio	Tracking Error	Information Ratio
			Panel A: Investment period Jul1998-Jun2008			
1a_6	9.3%	0.93	0.55	0.10	9.8%	0.95
1b_6	10.0%	0.82	0.62	0.12	10.9%	0.92
2a_6	13.2%	0.85	0.71	0.16	13.7%	0.97
2b_6	15.1%	0.76	0.84	0.20	14.2%	1.06
3a_6	14.8%	0.86	0.83	0.17	12.3%	1.20
3b_6	15.6%	0.73	0.92	0.21	13.4%	1.16
MIX6	6.2%	0.94	0.38	0.07	7.9%	0.77
			Panel B: Investment period Jul1998-Jun2003			
1a_6	9.5%	0.89	0.08	0.02	9.1%	1.05
1b_6	9.0%	0.75	0.13	0.03	11.3%	0.80
2a_6	11.7%	0.72	0.27	0.07	15.3%	0.77
2b_6	14.9%	0.60	0.52	0.16	16.2%	0.92
3a_6	12.3%	0.77	0.28	0.07	14.0%	0.88
3b_6	12.2%	0.60	0.38	0.11	15.9%	0.77
MIX6	2.9%	0.92	-0.29	-0.06	9.4%	0.30
			Panel C: Investment period Jul2003-Jun2008			
1a_6	7.9%	1.03	1.08	0.17	10.5%	0.75
1b_6	9.0%	0.98	1.15	0.18	10.6%	0.85
2a_6	10.8%	1.16	1.19	0.19	12.1%	0.90
2b_6	10.5%	1.14	1.17	0.18	12.1%	0.87
3a_6	14.8%	1.05	1.51	0.23	10.5%	1.41
3b_6	15.3%	1.00	1.55	0.24	10.5%	1.46
MIX6	9.2%	0.95	1.41	0.19	6.2%	1.49

Table 44: Performance measurement of investment strategies with fixed predictor variables – 6 style portfolios

Table 44 presents additional performance measures. Panel A covers the investment period Jul1998 to Jun2008. Panel B shows the evaluations for the subsample period Jul1998 to Jun2003 and Panel C exhibits the results for the subsample period Jul2003 to Jun2008. The calculations are based on monthly log excess returns covering the time period Jul1998 to Jun2008. The numbers are annualised wherever applicable. Calculations are conducted with reference to MKT where a benchmark is required.

All strategies show a considerable Jensen's Alpha. As we can see from Table 44, this holds for both of the subperiods. Over the entire investment period the Alpha is slightly higher in 3a_6 and 3b_6 than in 2a_6 and 2b_6, indicating a superior performance of the recursive window approach. However, the difference is small and may be within the range of estimation errors. In contrast, the rolling and recursive window strategies clearly exhibit a higher Alpha than strategies 1a_6 and 1b_6. Moreover, this is also true for the two subperiods, which supports the above finding of the importance of recalibrating the models after a certain time. In addition, all strategies present higher Alphas than MIX6. Hence, rotating among the six styles by the rules of the applied forecasting model beats a passive buy and hold portfolio consisting of the same styles. This can also be seen from the Sharpe Ratios or the

Treynor Ratios. However, the outperformance is accompanied by a considerable Tracking Error. Nevertheless, the Information Ratio of the active strategies is above the ratio of the benchmark portfolio during both subperiods and over the entire investment period.

Strategy	FF Alpha	Market Beta	Size Beta	Value Beta
Panel A: Investment period Jul1998-Jun2008				
1a_6	6.3% *	1.06 *	0.33 *	0.18 *
1b_6	6.3%	0.98 *	0.41 *	0.21 *
2a_6	5.9%	1.15 *	0.84 *	0.32 *
2b_6	8.1% *	1.05 *	0.79 *	0.32 *
3a_6	9.0% *	1.10 *	0.67 *	0.24 *
3b_6	9.4% *	0.99 *	0.70 *	0.29 *
MIX6	1.1%	1.15 *	0.57 *	0.23 *
Panel B: Investment period Jul1998-Jun2003				
1a_6	9.6% *	0.96 *	0.24 *	-0.01
1b_6	9.0% *	0.87 *	0.33 *	0.01
2a_6	11.1% *	1.08 *	0.81 *	0.26
2b_6	14.2% *	0.92 *	0.69 *	0.25
3a_6	12.5% *	1.00 *	0.67 *	0.02
3b_6	12.2% *	0.87 *	0.71 *	0.09
MIX6	2.5%	1.19 *	0.61 *	0.18 *
Panel C: Investment period Jul2003-Jun2008				
1a_6	1.5%	1.11 *	0.46 *	0.46 *
1b_6	2.2%	1.07 *	0.49 *	0.49 *
2a_6	-2.0%	1.32 *	0.91 *	0.31 *
2b_6	-2.6%	1.30 *	0.94 *	0.27
3a_6	5.7%	1.17 *	0.65 *	0.56 *
3b_6	6.2%	1.13 *	0.66 *	0.53 *
MIX6	1.6%	1.05 *	0.55 *	0.40 *

Table 45: Three-factor evaluation of investment strategies with fixed predictor variables – 6 style portfolios

Table 45 shows the results of a time series regression analysis with MKT and the two long-short portfolios SMB and HML as explanatory variables. Panel A covers the investment period Jul1998 to Jun2008. Panel B shows the evaluations for the subsample period Jul1998 to Jun2003 and Panel C provides the results for the subsample period Jul2003 to Jun2008.

$$P_{k,t} = a_k + b_k \cdot MKT_t + c_k \cdot SMB_t + d_k \cdot HML_t + \varepsilon$$

The monthly excess return $P_{k,t}$ of a portfolio k at t is regressed on the three factors MKT_t, SMB_t, and HML_t. The market beta is referred to as b_k, the size beta as c_k and the value beta as d_k. The constant, which is referred to as Fama-French Alpha (FF Alpha) is represented by a_k and shown as an annualised number. An asterisk indicates significance at the 5% level.

Jensen's Alpha might overlook certain risks, which may be a reason for the high returns of the active investment strategies. Hence, the strategies are also evaluated with the Fama-French Model. The results are presented in Table 45. The FF Alphas are clearly lower than the Jensen's Alphas. However, over the entire investment period a considerable Alpha remains in each of the active strategies. In other words, the returns of the active investment strategies followed cannot be entirely explained by the Fama-French Model. Interestingly, as Panels B and C show, Alphas are, in particular significant during the first half of the investment period. Hence, it seems that forecasting is more appealing in times of negative aggregate market returns.

The above evaluations also reveal additional insights into the sources of the high returns of some strategies. For instance, strategies 2a_6 and 2b_6 show a substantial exposure to *SMB* and *HML*; thus, the high returns might also be associated with risks not captured by the CAPM. These high exposures and the non-significance of the Alphas during the second half of the investment period might raise some doubts about the forecasting power of the models. However, the mixed evidence is attributable to the second half of the investment period when Alphas turned insignificant. This again raises the question whether market participants exploited market inefficiencies or if the low Alphas are a particularity of a certain time period.

Strategy	MKT_RF < 0	MKT_RF > 0	MIX6_RF < 0	MIX6_RF > 0
	Investment period: Jul1998-Jun2008			
1a_6	-3.3%	3.6%	-3.4%	3.4%
1b_6	-2.8%	3.3%	-3.0%	3.2%
2a_6	-2.6%	3.7%	-3.5%	4.0%
2b_6	-2.1%	3.6%	-2.9%	3.9%
3a_6	-2.6%	3.9%	-3.3%	4.1%
3b_6	-2.0%	3.6%	-2.7%	3.8%
MKT	-4.0%	2.8%	-3.7%	2.3%
MIX6	-3.2%	3.1%	-4.1%	3.4%

Table 46: Conditional mean excess returns of investment strategies with fixed predictor variables – 6 style portfolios
Table 46 presents the mean log excess returns of the investment strategies under the condition that the log excess return of MKT or MIX6 is negative (MKT_RF < 0, MIX6_RF < 0) or positive (MKT_RF > 0, MIX6_RF > 0). The calculations are based on monthly data.

The negative MKT months have on average a log excess return of -4.0%. During the same months all active investment strategies as wells as MIX6 have a higher log excess return, which we can see from Table 46. Moreover, all active strategies and MIX6 beat the market on average in months with positive MKT returns. The evidence is similar when the returns of MIX6 are taken as the condition. On average, over all negative months of MIX6, it had a return of -4.1%. During the same months, all active investment strategies had a higher average log excess return. The picture is slightly different for the positive MIX6 months. On average, over all positive months of MIX6 it had a return of 3.4%. During the same months MKT and Strategy 1b_6 had a lower average return, and all other strategies show equal or higher excess returns. In other words, five of six strategies had on average higher returns in downside as well as in upside months of MIX6. Moreover, this is not entirely a result of a few very strong months during negative months of MIX6, as is outlined in more detail below.

Strategy	Minus Months	Conditional MMs	Detected
	Investment period: Jul1998-Jun2008		
1a_6	49	38	
1b_6	41	31	15
2a_6	43	36	
2b_6	34	28	18
3a_6	44	37	
3b_6	34	27	19
MIX6	46	46	

Table 47: Unconditional and conditional number of negative log excess returns of investment strategies with fixed predictor variables – 6 style portfolios
Table 47 presents the number of monthly negative log excess returns for each of the strategies which are based on fixed predictor variables as well as for the benchmark MIX6. The number of unconditional negative excess returns is listed in the column Minus Months. The number of conditional negative excess returns is shown in the column Conditional MMs. The condition is a negative excess return of MIX6 in the respective month. The number of correctly predicted negative returns is shown in the column Detected.

Table 47 provides further evidence on the forecasting performance of the applied models. For example, MIX6 had 46 months with negative log excess returns and Strategy 2b_6 had 34 months with negative log excess returns. Hence, over the entire investment period Strategy 2b_6 had 12 fewer months with negative excess returns than the benchmark portfolios MIX6. However, the intersection totals only 28 months. In other words, during the 46 negative months of MIX6, Strategy 2b_6 had 28 months which were also negative. The difference of 18 months can be interpreted as correctly forecasted negative excess returns. In those months Strategy 2b_6 invested in the fixed income instrument or in a portfolio with a positive excess return. However, there are 6 months in which the strategy had a negative excess return but the benchmark return was positive.

7.6.2. Changing Predictor Portfolios

In the following I investigate how a change in the predictor variables at Jun2003 affects the results of the investment strategies. The approach is the same as for the strategies with the restricted IOS. I rely on the estimated lead-lag relationships from section 6.1. As the lead-lag relationships change over time, it may be of interest to replace the incumbent predictor variables with other portfolios. Recall that the length of the interval after which an investor checks for superior predictors can be chosen arbitrarily. I again apply an interval of 60 months, which equals the length of the subsample periods. As in the previous section, the investment period starts with Jul1998. The returns of the period Jul1998 to Jun2003 are forecasted with the same models as above, and a long position in the portfolio with the highest forecasted return is taken. In Jun2003 the investor tests for superior forecasting power of other portfolios. In other words, in Jun2003 the lead-lag relationships of the past 60 months are considered. Then, for each of the combined style portfolios SH, SM, SL, BH, BM, and BL, the portfolio with the highest (cross-)serial correlation coefficient is chosen as the predictor portfolio.

$$
\begin{aligned}
&SH\_RF_t = \alpha_{SH} + \phi_{SH} BH\_RF_{t-1} + \varepsilon_t \\
&SM\_RF_t = \alpha_{SM} + \phi_{SM} BH\_RF_{t-1} + \varepsilon_t \\
&SL\_RF_t = \alpha_{SL} + \phi_{SL} BH\_RF_{t-1} + \varepsilon_t \\
&BH\_RF_t = \alpha_{BH} + \phi_{BH} BH\_RF_{t-1} + \varepsilon_t \\
&BM\_RF_t = \alpha_{BM} + \phi_{BM} BH\_RF_{t-1} + \varepsilon_t \\
&BL\_RF_t = \alpha_{BL} + \phi_{BL} BH\_RF_{t-1} + \varepsilon_t
\end{aligned} \tag{51}
$$

(51) shows the models which are calibrated the first time with data from Jul1993 to Jun1998. These are the same models as in the previous section. However, in Jun2003 the investor checks for better models with data from Jul1998 to Jun2003.

$$(52)\quad \begin{aligned} SH\_RF_t &= \alpha_{SH} + \phi_{SH} BL\_RF_{t-1} + \varepsilon_t \\ SM\_RF_t &= \alpha_{SM} + \phi_{SM} SM\_RF_{t-1} + \varepsilon_t \\ SL\_RF_t &= \alpha_{SL} + \phi_{SL} GROWTH\_RF_{t-1} + \varepsilon_t \\ BH\_RF_t &= \alpha_{BH} + \phi_{BH} GROWTH\_RF_{t-1} + \varepsilon_t \\ BM\_RF_t &= \alpha_{BM} + \phi_{BM} BL\_RF_{t-1} + \varepsilon_t \\ BL\_RF_t &= \alpha_{BL} + \phi_{BL} BL\_RF_{t-1} + \varepsilon_t \end{aligned}$$

Table 18 in section 6.1. shows the lead-lag relationships of the period Jul1998 to Jun2003. For each of the six Fama-French Portfolios the one with the highest (cross-)autocorrelation coefficient is used as the predictor for the next 60 months. The models are shown in (52).

Strategy	IOS	Calibration Method	Calibration Window	Investment Period
4a_6	SH, SM, SL, BH, BM, BL	Once with change	60 months	Jul1998-Jun2008
4b_6	SH, SM, SL, BH, BM, BL, LIBOR	Once with change	60 months	Jul1998-Jun2008
5a_6	SH, SM, SL, BH, BM, BL	Rolling with change	60 months	Jul1998-Jun2008
5b_6	SH, SM, SL, BH, BM, BL, LIBOR	Rolling with change	60 months	Jul1998-Jun2008
6a_6	SH, SM, SL, BH, BM, BL	Recursive with change	60 months*	Jul1998-Jun2008
6b_6	SH, SM, SL, BH, BM, BL, LIBOR	Recursive with change	60 months*	Jul1998-Jun2008

Table 48: Investment strategies with changing predictor variables – 6 style portfolios
Table 48 shows some key characteristics of the investment strategies which apply a changing predictor portfolio. There are three times two strategies which differ with respect to the calibration method. For each strategy, there is an alternative with a possible fixed income investment. The calibration period for the recursive window refers to the initial estimation period. Then, the window increases, which is indicated by *.

Table 48 shows the basic characteristics of strategies 4a_6 to 6b_6. The only difference to the strategies of the previous section is the replacement of the predictor portfolio at Jun2003. Hence, the models of the first half of the investment period are identical to those of strategies 1a_6 to 3b_6.

Strategy	# Transactions	Total Return	Mean (annualised)	Risk (annualised)
Panel A: Investment period Jul1998-Jun2008				
4a_6	71	317.2%	14.3%	17.3%
4b_6	85	258.5%	12.8%	16.5%
5a_6	73	350.3%	15.0%	18.5%
5b_6	82	455.3%	17.1%	17.9%
6a_6	75	388.4%	15.9%	17.5%
6b_6	80	397.5%	16.0%	16.7%
MKT	-	17.5%	1.6%	15.0%
MIX6	-	117.1%	7.8%	16.2%
Panel B: Investment period Jul1998-Jun2003				
4a_6	29	18.0%	3.3%	18.0%
4b_6	42	22.0%	4.0%	16.8%
5a_6	29	41.9%	7.0%	19.1%
5b_6	38	75.3%	11.2%	18.0%
6a_6	33	42.7%	7.1%	19.1%
6b_6	37	53.6%	8.6%	17.8%
MKT	-	-30.3%	-7.2%	17.6%
MIX6	-	-16.7%	-3.6%	18.7%
Panel C: Investment period Jul2003-Jun2008				
4a_6	42	253.7%	25.3%	16.2%
4b_6	43	193.9%	21.6%	15.9%
5a_6	44	217.3%	23.1%	17.8%
5b_6	44	216.8%	23.1%	17.8%
6a_6	42	242.4%	24.6%	15.5%
6b_6	43	223.9%	23.5%	15.4%
MKT	-	68.4%	10.4%	11.6%
MIX6	-	160.6%	19.2%	12.6%

Table 49: Risk and return of investment strategies with changing predictor variables – 6 style portfolios
The above table presents basic evaluations of the previously described investment strategies and the market as well as MIX6. Panel A covers the investment period Jul1998 to Jun2008. Panel B shows the evaluations for the subsample period Jul1998 to Jun2003 and Panel C displays the results for the subsample period Jul2003 to Jun2008. The number of transactions represents the number of switches between the four styles. Total returns are calculated with gross returns. The annual mean return and the standard deviation (Risk) are based on log returns.

In terms of total return, it seems favourable to adjust the predictor variables after the first half of the investment period. By comparing Panel C of Table 49 to Panel C of Table 42, we can see that investment strategies which are based on forecasting models with changing predictor variables have a higher return in four out of six strategies. The two strategies with a recursive window approach underperform their counterparts with fixed forecasting variables. However, the risk expressed as standard deviation seems to be comparable to the strategies evaluated in the previous section.

Strategy	SH	SM	SL	BH	BM	BL	LIBOR
Panel A: Investment period Jul1998-Jun2008							
4a_6	13	12	36	17	0	42	0
4b_6	10	12	36	14	0	32	16
5a_6	34	12	42	19	0	13	0
5b_6	25	12	42	18	0	11	12
6a_6	30	17	47	5	0	21	0
6b_6	24	17	47	4	0	14	14
Panel B: Investment period Jul1998-Jun2003							
4a_6	0	0	8	11	0	41	0
4b_6	0	0	8	11	0	32	9
5a_6	17	3	16	11	0	13	0
5b_6	8	3	16	11	0	11	11
6a_6	13	4	21	2	0	20	0
6b_6	8	4	21	2	0	14	11
Panel C: Investment period Jul2003-Jun2008							
4a_6	13	12	28	6	0	1	0
4b_6	10	12	28	3	0	0	7
5a_6	17	9	26	8	0	0	0
5b_6	17	9	26	7	0	0	1
6a_6	17	13	26	3	0	1	0
6b_6	16	13	26	2	0	0	3

Table 50: Allocation of funds during investment period – changing predictor variables and 6 style portfolios

Table 50 shows the number of months in which each strategy was invested in a particular style portfolio. Panel A covers the investment period Jul1998 to Jun2008. Panel B shows the evaluations for the subsample period Jul1998 to Jun2003 and Panel C provides the results for the subsample period Jul2003 to Jun2008. For example, over the entire investment period Strategy 4b_6 was invested 10 months in small value stocks (SH), 12 months in small neutral stocks (SM), 36 months in small growth stocks (SL), 14 months in large value stocks (BH), 32 months in large growth stocks (BL), and 16 months in the fixed income instrument (LIBOR).

Replacing the predictor variables affects the allocation of the funds. For instance, Panel C of Table 50 exhibits a more frequent allocation to SM across all strategies. Moreover, strategies 4a_6 and 4b_6 are now also invested in small value stocks. This was not the case in strategies 1a_6 and 1b_6. Moreover, there are also more frequent investments in small growth stocks in strategies 4a_6 and 4b_6 than in 1a_6 and 1b_6.

Strategy	Jensen's Alpha	CAPM Beta	Sharpe Ratio	Treynor Ratio	Tracking Error	Information Ratio
			Panel A: Investment period Jul1998-Jun2008			
4a_6	12.7%	0.93	0.73	0.14	10.3%	1.23
4b_6	11.2%	0.83	0.68	0.14	11.2%	1.00
5a_6	13.5%	0.84	0.73	0.16	13.9%	0.97
5b_6	15.6%	0.75	0.87	0.21	14.4%	1.08
6a_6	14.3%	0.82	0.82	0.18	12.8%	1.12
6b_6	14.5%	0.69	0.87	0.21	13.9%	1.04
MIX6	6.2%	0.94	0.38	0.07	7.9%	0.77
			Panel B: Investment period Jul1998-Jun2003			
4a_6	9.5%	0.89	0.08	0.02	9.1%	1.05
4b_6	9.0%	0.75	0.13	0.03	11.3%	0.80
5a_6	11.7%	0.72	0.27	0.07	15.3%	0.77
5b_6	14.9%	0.60	0.52	0.16	16.2%	0.92
6a_6	12.3%	0.77	0.28	0.07	14.0%	0.88
6b_6	12.2%	0.60	0.38	0.11	15.9%	0.77
MIX6	2.9%	0.92	-0.29	-0.06	9.4%	0.30
			Panel C: Investment period Jul2003-Jun2008			
4a_6	14.9%	1.00	1.47	0.24	11.4%	1.31
4b_6	11.4%	0.98	1.27	0.21	11.2%	1.01
5a_6	11.7%	1.10	1.22	0.20	12.4%	0.94
5b_6	11.7%	1.10	1.22	0.20	12.4%	0.94
6a_6	15.1%	0.90	1.50	0.26	11.5%	1.32
6b_6	14.3%	0.87	1.44	0.26	11.8%	1.21
MIX6	9.2%	0.95	1.41	0.19	6.2%	1.49

Table 51: Performance measurement of investment strategies with changing predictor variables – 6 style portfolios
Table 51 presents additional performance measures. Panel A covers the investment period Jul1998 to Jun2008. Panel B shows the evaluations for the subsample period Jul1998 to Jun2003 and Panel C presents the results for the subsample period Jul2003 to Jun2008. The calculations are based on monthly log excess returns covering the time period Jul1998 to Jun2008. The numbers are annualised wherever applicable. Calculations are conducted with reference to MKT where a benchmark is required.

The highest deviations compared to the investment strategies with fixed predictor variables can be found in 4a_6 and 4b_6 when they are compared to 1a_6 and 1b_6. Most notably, as we can see from Panel C of Table 51, Jensen's Alpha is higher for the strategies with a replacement of the forecasting variables. However, I am aware of the possibility that a simple recalibration of the models underlying 4a_6 and 4b_6 might have a similar effect as a replacement of the predictor variables.

Strategy	FF Alpha	Market Beta	Size Beta	Value Beta
		Panel A: Investment period Jul1998-Jun2008		
4a_6	8.0% *	1.12 *	0.53 *	0.22 *
4b_6	6.1% *	1.03 *	0.58 *	0.20 *
5a_6	5.4%	1.17 *	0.91 *	0.40 *
5b_6	7.8% *	1.08 *	0.85 *	0.42 *
6a_6	7.7% *	1.07 *	0.79 *	0.18 *
6b_6	7.4% *	0.97 *	0.83 *	0.25 *
MIX6	1.1%	1.15 *	0.57 *	0.23 *
		Panel B: Investment period Jul1998-Jun2003		
4a_6	9.6% *	0.96 *	0.24 *	-0.01
4b_6	9.0% *	0.87 *	0.33 *	0.01
5a_6	11.1% *	1.08 *	0.81 *	0.26
5b_6	14.2% *	0.92 *	0.69 *	0.25
6a_6	12.5% *	1.00 *	0.67 *	0.02
6b_6	12.2% *	0.87 *	0.71 *	0.09
MIX6	2.5%	1.19 *	0.61 *	0.18 *
		Panel C: Investment period Jul2003-Jun2008		
4a_6	1.9%	1.16 *	0.93 *	0.55 *
4b_6	-1.5%	1.14 *	0.92 *	0.43 *
5a_6	-3.3%	1.30 *	1.07 *	0.57 *
5b_6	-3.3%	1.30 *	1.08 *	0.57 *
6a_6	0.8%	1.09 *	1.02 *	0.46 *
6b_6	0.0%	1.05 *	1.02 *	0.47 *
MIX6	1.6%	1.05 *	0.55 *	0.40 *

Table 52: Three-factor evaluation of investment strategies with changing predictor variables – 6 style portfolios

Table 52 shows the results of a time series regression analysis with MKT and the two long-short portfolios SMB and HML as explanatory variables. Panel A covers the investment period Jul1998 to Jun2008. Panel B shows the evaluations for the subsample period Jul1998 to Jun2003 and Panel C displays the results for the subsample period Jul2003 to Jun2008.

$$P_{k,t} = a_k + b_k \cdot MKT_t + c_k \cdot SMB_t + d_k \cdot HML_t + \varepsilon$$

The monthly excess return $P_{k,t}$ of a portfolio k at t is regressed on the three factors MKT_t, SMB_t, and HML_t. The market beta is referred to as b_k, the size beta as c_k and the value beta as d_k. The constant, which is referred to as Fama-French Alpha (FF Alpha), is represented by a_k and shown as an annualised number. An asterisk indicates significance at the 5% level.

As there is no change in the first subperiod, we can focus on Panel C of Table 52. The FF Alphas are lower in five of the six active investment strategies if we compare the values to those of the previous section. Changing the predictors seems to cause higher exposures to the Fama-French Factors, which is rewarded with a higher return but not an outperformance in terms of FF Alpha. In particular, strategies 4a_6 and 4b_6 show a considerable increase in the exposure to SMB, which may be one reason for the higher total return compared to 1a_6 and 1b_6. Adjusting the predictor variable might cause forecasts based on portfolios which had high (cross-)serial correlations during the more recent past. This seems especially unappealing in times of bubbles as a potentially rational serial correlation or lead-lag relationship may be dominated by irrational relationships such as extreme autocorrelation in a particular market segment.

Strategy	MKT_RF < 0	MKT_RF > 0	MIX6_RF < 0	MIX6_RF > 0
	Investment period: Jul1998-Jun2008			
4a_6	-3.1%	3.9%	-3.3%	3.8%
4b_6	-2.7%	3.5%	-3.0%	3.4%
5a_6	-2.5%	3.6%	-3.5%	4.0%
5b_6	-2.1%	3.6%	-3.0%	4.0%
6a_6	-2.3%	3.6%	-3.1%	3.9%
6b_6	-1.9%	3.4%	-2.7%	3.6%
MKT	-4.0%	2.8%	-3.7%	2.3%
MIX6	-3.2%	3.1%	-4.1%	3.4%

Table 53: Conditional mean excess returns of investment strategies with changing predictor variables – 6 style portfolios
Table 53 presents the mean log excess returns of the investment strategies under the condition that the log excess return of MKT or MIX6 is negative (MKT_RF < 0, MIX6_RF < 0) or positive (MKT_RF > 0, MIX6_RF > 0). The calculations are based on monthly data.

With respect to their conditional performance, strategies 4a_6 to 6b_6 do not seem to be considerably superior to their counterparts 1a_6 to 3b_6. This can be seen by comparing Tables 53 and 54 to Tables 46 and 47. For instance, Strategy 5a_6 has an average log excess return of -2.5% over the months with negative log excess returns of MKT. Its counterpart with fixed predictor variable, Strategy 2a_6, has an average log excess return of -2.6%. Similar differences hold for the remainder of the strategies. Moreover, the differences are also very close in months with positive returns of MKT or in the case conditional on the returns of MIX6.

Strategy	Minus Months	Conditional MMs	Detected
	Investment period: Jul1998-Jun2008		
4a_6	45	37	
4b_6	39	32	14
5a_6	40	35	
5b_6	33	29	17
6a_6	41	35	
6b_6	34	28	18
MIX6	46	46	

Table 54: Unconditional and conditional number of negative log excess returns of investment strategies with changing predictor variables – 6 style portfolios
Table 54 presents the number of monthly negative log excess returns for each of the strategies which are based on changing predictor variables as well as for the benchmark MIX6. The number of unconditional negative excess returns is listed in the column Minus Months. The number of conditional negative excess returns is shown in the column Conditional MMs. The condition is a negative excess return of MIX6 in the respective month. The number of correctly predicted negative returns is shown in the column Detected.

Interestingly, all strategies with changing predictor variables have equal or fewer months with negative excess returns than the strategies with fixed predictor portfolios. In contrast, the "detection rate" is a little lower. Hence, the lower number of negative months might be compensated by a weaker forecasting power.

7.7. Summary of Empirical Part II

The present chapter introduces two groups of style rotation strategies. The first group applies an IOS of the four style portfolios SMALL, BIG, VALUE, GROWTH. The second group applies the six Fama-French Portfolios SH,…,BL as IOS. These two IOS groups are separated into two subgroups which apply either fixed or changing predictor variables in their forecasting models. In addition, the forecasting models are calibrated by three different approaches. Finally, an alternative of each strategy allows for a fixed income instrument.

The investment strategies presented are based on the forecasting models outlined in Chapter 6. The success of the investment strategies is evaluated over the 10-year period Jul1998 to Jun2008 as well as over the two 60-month periods Jul1998 to Jun2003 and Jul2003 to Jun2008. Several performance measures such as the Sharpe Ratio or the Treynor Ratio are applied. In addition, a multi-factor approach is used in order to identify a potential outperformance after accounting for risks not captured by the CAPM.

Almost all active investment strategies considered beat the market as well as a style-based benchmark portfolio with respect to “classic” performance measures such as the Sharpe Ratio. The application of a multi-factor model puts the outperformance into perspective. However, there are several investment strategies which exhibit a significant outperformance. The most pronounced outperformance in terms of FF Alpha amounts to 9.4% on an annualised basis and can be found in the group with the six Fama-French Portfolios as IOS. The significant FF Alphas are supported by the risk-adjusted excess returns of Arshanapalli, Switzer, and Panju (2007) for style rotation strategies based on US data.

The finer separation of the four style portfolios into six market segments is associated with higher total returns as well as higher FF Alphas. While the higher total returns might be due to a higher exposure to certain risk factors, the higher FF Alphas may be attributed to more accurate forecasts for finer market segments. Moreover, the possibility of investments in a fixed income instrument increases the FF Alphas rather than it decreases them.

With the entire investment period in view, the hypothesis that a passive buy and hold portfolio beats the active investment strategies might be rejected. However, the evidence on the two subperiods is mixed. While the first half of the investment period revealed significant positive FF Alphas, the evaluations of the second half of the investment period shows diminishing significance of the FF Alphas. Moreover, even negative Alphas appear. However, significance is also associated with sample size, which is restricted to 60 months for the two subsample periods.

8. Conclusion

8.1. Summary of Findings

Lo and MacKinlay (1989; 1990a; 1990b) report strong serial correlation in the returns of small cap portfolios. In addition, they find large caps leading small caps. The double ranking of Fama and French (1992) allows a closer look at serial correlation of style portfolios. The two groups large caps and small caps can be separated into six finer market segments which match a size criterion as well as a valuation criterion. Based on these six market segments or combined styles, Fama and French (1993-1998) introduce two new risk factors which may be able to capture risks associated with changes in the real economy. In parallel, Boudoukh, Richardson, and Whitelaw (1994) introduce the concept of implied cross-autocorrelation, which enables a breakdown of cross-autocorrelation into serial correlation and contemporaneous correlation.

The concept of implied cross-autocorrelation leads to tests of the random walk model and is useful in order to answer the first research question of whether or not the returns of the Fama-French Portfolios are applicable in stock return forecasting. Both, autocorrelation coefficients and a heteroskedasticity-consistent test based on variance ratios, are applied in order to test the random walk model. With monthly data ranging from Jul1993 to Jun2008, serial correlation appears in the returns of various portfolios. Among the six Fama-French Portfolios significant serial correlation can be found in large value stocks, large neutral stocks, small neutral stocks, and small growth stocks. Over the entire sample period all style-based portfolios as well as the market index, MKT, exhibit significant first-order serial correlation. The autocorrelation is positive in all of the previously mentioned portfolios. The strongest autocorrelation is found in the returns of small caps. This is supported by the findings of Lo and MacKinlay (1988), Mech (1993), and others. Of the two long-short portfolios only SMB shows significant autocorrelation over the full sample period. The only case with significant negative serial correlation appears in the returns of HML during the first subsample period. Serial correlation seems to be less significant in each of the subperiods. In the last subperiod none of the portfolios shows significant first-order serial correlation. However, regression analyses revealed small caps to exhibit considerable coefficient values until mid-2007. The variance ratio tests mostly confirm the findings of the autocorrelation analyses. First-order serial correlation seems to be nothing unusual over the entire sample period and in the first two subsample periods, which cover the time period Jul1993 to Jun2003. However, accounting for heteroskedasticity clearly lowers the significance of the serial correlation. Moreover, serial correlation in aggregate market returns disappears. This points to a certain influence of time-varying volatility and highlights the possibility of uncorrelated aggregate market returns but serially correlated returns of some (combined) style portfolios.

Taking into account the overall evidence suggests a rejection of the null hypothesis that the returns of the Fama-French Portfolios follow a random walk. Moreover, serial correlation seems to change over time. Returns of a particular portfolio might be serially uncorrelated in one period but show autocorrelation during another period. However, the positive serial correlation in the returns of large value stocks and the average small cap seem to be relatively consistent. Nevertheless, the vanishing autocorrelation during the last sample period raises the question of whether serial correlation in the returns of certain (combined) style portfolios has been exploited by market participants or if it is a particularity of the most recent time period.

The second research question stated in the introduction targets the economic relevance and significance of (cross-)serial correlation. In the course of testing for profitable investment strategies, two groups of style rotation strategies are introduced. These investment strategies are based on forecasting models which also allow for models relying on empirical cross-autocorrelation. The first group of strategies applies an IOS of the four style portfolios SMALL, BIG, VALUE, and GROWTH. The second group of strategies applies the six Fama-French Portfolios SH,...,BL as IOS. These two IOS groups are further separated into two subgroups which apply either fixed or changing predictor variables. Several performance measures such as the Sharpe Ratio or the Treynor Ratio are applied. In addition, a multi-factor approach is used in order to identify a potential outperformance after accounting for (cyclical) risks not captured by the CAPM. Almost all of the active investment strategies considered beat the market as well as a style based benchmark portfolio with respect to "classic" performance measures such as the Sharpe Ratio. The application of a multi-factor model puts the outperformance into perspective; however, there are several investment strategies which exhibit a significant outperformance. The most pronounced outperformance in terms of FF Alpha amounts to 9.4% on an annualised basis and can be found in the group with the six Fama-French Portfolios as IOS. The significant FF Alphas are supported by the risk-adjusted excess returns of Arshanapalli, Switzer, and Panju (2007) for style rotation strategies based on US data.

The finer separation of the four style portfolios into six market segments is associated with higher total returns as well as higher FF Alphas. While the higher total returns might be due to a higher exposure to certain risk factors, the higher FF Alphas may be attributed to more accurate forecasts for finer market segments. Moreover, the possibility of investments in a fixed income instrument increases rather than decreases the FF Alphas. With the entire investment period in view, the hypothesis that a passive buy and hold portfolio beats the active investment strategies might be rejected. However, the evidence on the two subperiods is mixed. While the first half of the investment period reveals significant positive FF Alphas, the evaluations of the second half of the investment period shows diminishing significance of the FF Alphas.

Overall, my research supports the evidence on significant serial correlation in the returns of various market segments. The most challenging question might be where the the significant serial correlation comes from. Boudoukh, Richardson, and Whitelaw (1994) mention three possible explanations. The first, market frictions, seems unappealing. Lo and MacKinlay (1990b) find market frictions to account only for a small part of the autocorrelation. In addition, the above-evaluated returns are value weighted. Hence, even in the small cap portfolios the largest stocks are the most dominant. The second explanation, a partial adjustment to new information, seems more appealing and is supported by a number of researchers such as Brennan, Jegadeesh, and Swaminathan (1993) or Chordia and Swaminathan (2000). The third explanation, time-varying risk premia, might also be a reasonable source of serial correlation in returns. This view is supported by, among others, Fama and French (1989), Hameed (1997), and Perez-Quiros and Timmermann (2000). With the two risk factors SMB and HML and the growing body of research on cyclical risks in view, I offer an explanation based on time-varying risk premia.

Besides the market risk there might be cyclical risks associated with the real economy. Cochrane (1999a) argues that SMB and HML may capture such risks. The above evidence shows high serial correlation in the returns of certain small cap portfolios as well as in the returns of large value stocks. These portfolios have high exposures to SMB or HML, i.e., cyclical risks. Thus, small caps and value stocks might be traded at low prices during recessions as only a few investors are willing or able to hold such stocks. As business activity accelerates and the prospects of these companies improve, the prices increase. This cyclical improvement of business conditions might cause a more or less gradual decrease of the risk premia associated with the real economy, which results in serial correlation. Balvers, Cosimano, and McDonald (1990) argue that aggregate output is serially correlated, which causes stock returns to be serially correlated as well. Recent research pointing to the possibility of risk premia associated with the macroeconomic environment supports this argument. In other words, there may be a risk premium which is high in recessions and low during economic expansion. This is a separate risk premium from the market risk premium. This cyclical risk premium diminishes as the macroeconomic situation improves. The decreasing risk premium drives up the stock prices in such a way that returns of recession-sensitive market segments exhibit serial correlation.

We might get a clearer picture if we, as Cochrane (1999b) suggests, look at the stock market as a big insurance market. In a recession the risk premia for cyclical risks may be high, which means low prices for stocks which have high exposure to movements in the real economy. Investors who are no longer willing or able to hold the stocks which show poor returns in bad times will sell their stocks. The seller of the stocks buys protection against the worst case: A loss of his job or business at the same time as his stocks become worthless. On the other side, there is a buyer. This must be a person or institution which is able to bear the risks associated with a deteriorating macroeconomic environment. The buyer of the stocks sells insurance to the seller of the stocks. In return, the buyer receives a risk premium. The situation of the investor who sold the stocks may change as the macroeconomic environment effectively improves. His job is safer again and the worst case is more distant. Hence, more investors become able to hold stocks exposed to cyclical risks, which lowers the risk premium. Such a time-varying ability of taking cyclical risks may cause serial correlation in the returns of various market segments and does not contradict efficient markets.

8.2. Implications for Practice

The above-presented empirical findings on serial correlation and the explanation offered for its source may be of particular interest for portfolio managers and financial analysts. The investigations of serial correlation show that the random walk model might be a reasonable approximation for aggregate market returns. However, the rejection of the random walk model for several market segments requires attention in many investment decisions.

High serial correlation in the returns of certain market segments could indicate a non-trivial exposure to cyclical risks. In portfolio management, this exposure should be matched to an investor's risk profile. However, exposure to cyclical risks might be well known if a multi-factor model is applied in performance evaluation. In contrast, there are aspects which are less obvious. First and foremost, serial correlation, which is not accounted for in Modern Portfolio Theory, increases the variance of multi-period returns more strongly than expected by multiplying the variance of single period returns. Therefore, an appropriate risk management approach is required. This might be especially true for style-based investment strategies.

Similar implications hold for financial analysis. For instance, the determination of cost of capital is directly impacted by serial correlation. Companies in market segments with high serial correlation may face time-varying risk premia for cyclical risks. Therefore, the estimation period for the cost of capital becomes crucial and the time horizon of an investment project becomes more relevant. In sum, the implications of serial correlation call for more sophisticated risk management approaches and a review of the random walk model in many of its applications within the area of finance.

8.3. Research Outlook

The research presented in this book is based on data for the Swiss stock market and is limited to a time period in the recent past. Hence, a natural extension would be to test the random walk model on a market segment level for other countries. Moreover, as time passes and more data becomes available, it may be appropriate to revisit the evidence on the Swiss stock market. I would also suggest the investigation of serial correlation on the industry level as such an analysis might reveal more information on the link between autocorrelation and the changing states of the real economy.

Investigations conditional on the state of the economy might also be helpful with respect to a more thorough understanding of return predictability and its relationship to business activity. For instance, it may be that serial correlation is high during an expansion of the economy but low during its contraction. In addition, as shown in Fama and French (2007b), a decomposition of returns into dividend yield, growth of book value, and growth of the price-to-book ratio seems to be an interesting refinement. This break down of returns would help to better understand the source of serial correlation. Other extensions of my research could point in the direction of applications in portfolio management and financial analysis.

Appendix

A1. Variance Ratios (q=4)

Portfolio	VR(4)	Psi(4)	Psi*(4)
	Jul1993-Jun2008		
SH_RF	1.33	2.40	2.09
SM_RF	1.72	5.18	4.47
SL_RF	1.73	5.20	3.13
BH_RF	1.64	4.59	4.02
BM_RF	1.27	1.94	1.26
BL_RF	1.31	2.24	1.92
SMB	1.19	1.37	1.28
HML	0.96	-0.28	-0.24
MKT_RF	1.35	2.54	2.14
SPI_RF	1.30	2.14	1.52
SMALL_RF	1.70	5.04	3.92
BIG_RF	1.53	3.79	2.71
VALUE_RF	1.62	4.44	3.98
GROWTH_RF	1.62	4.47	3.18

Table 55: Variance ratios and test statistics (q=4) – full sample
The above table shows the variance ratios and two test statistics for the six Fama-French Portfolios, SMALL, BIG, VALUE, GROWTH, MKT, and the Swiss Performance Index. The variance ratios are shown in the column marked VR(4). The biased test statistic is shown in the column denoted Psi(4). The corrected test statistic which accounts for heteroskedasticity is presented in the column marked Psi*(4). The variance ratios are calculated by using four period returns, which is indicated by (4).

Portfolio	Jul1993-Jun1998			Jul1998-Jun2003			Jul2003-Jun2008		
	VR(4)	Psi(4)	Psi*(4)	VR(4)	Psi(4)	Psi*(4)	VR(4)	Psi(4)	Psi*(4)
SH_RF	1.30	1.23	0.98	1.03	0.14	0.14	1.51	2.11	2.24
SM_RF	1.64	2.65	2.43	1.67	2.76	2.57	1.43	1.78	1.76
SL_RF	1.24	1.01	1.00	1.90	3.74	2.84	0.96	-0.17	-0.14
BH_RF	2.05	4.33	4.44	1.47	1.94	1.71	1.30	1.23	1.38
BM_RF	1.52	2.15	2.09	0.88	-0.49	-0.39	1.44	1.80	1.89
BL_RF	1.16	0.67	0.61	1.01	0.06	0.05	1.43	1.80	1.76
SMB	1.03	0.12	0.10	1.29	1.21	1.23	1.07	0.28	0.25
HML	0.53	-1.96	-1.77	1.20	0.81	0.72	1.11	0.45	0.46
MKT_RF	1.23	0.96	0.85	1.02	0.08	0.07	1.48	2.00	2.05
SPI_RF	1.28	1.14	1.05	0.93	-0.29	-0.21	1.45	1.86	1.90
SMALL_RF	1.57	2.36	2.15	1.71	2.95	2.56	1.27	1.13	1.03
BIG_RF	1.87	3.60	3.45	1.08	0.35	0.28	1.47	1.93	2.14
VALUE_RF	1.89	3.67	3.59	1.28	1.16	1.07	1.46	1.90	2.07
GROWTH_RF	1.28	1.16	1.05	1.66	2.71	2.26	1.13	0.55	0.54

Table 56: Variance ratios and test statistics (q=4) – subsamples
The above table shows the variance ratios and two test statistics for the six Fama-French Portfolios, SMALL, BIG, VALUE, GROWTH, MKT, and the Swiss Performance Index. The variance ratios are shown in the column marked VR(4). The biased test statistic is shown in the column denoted Psi(4). The corrected test statistic which accounts for heteroskedasticity is presented in the column marked Psi*(4). The variance ratios are calculated by using four period returns, which is indicated by (4).

A2. Style Rotation Strategies (1a to 3b) vs. SMALL

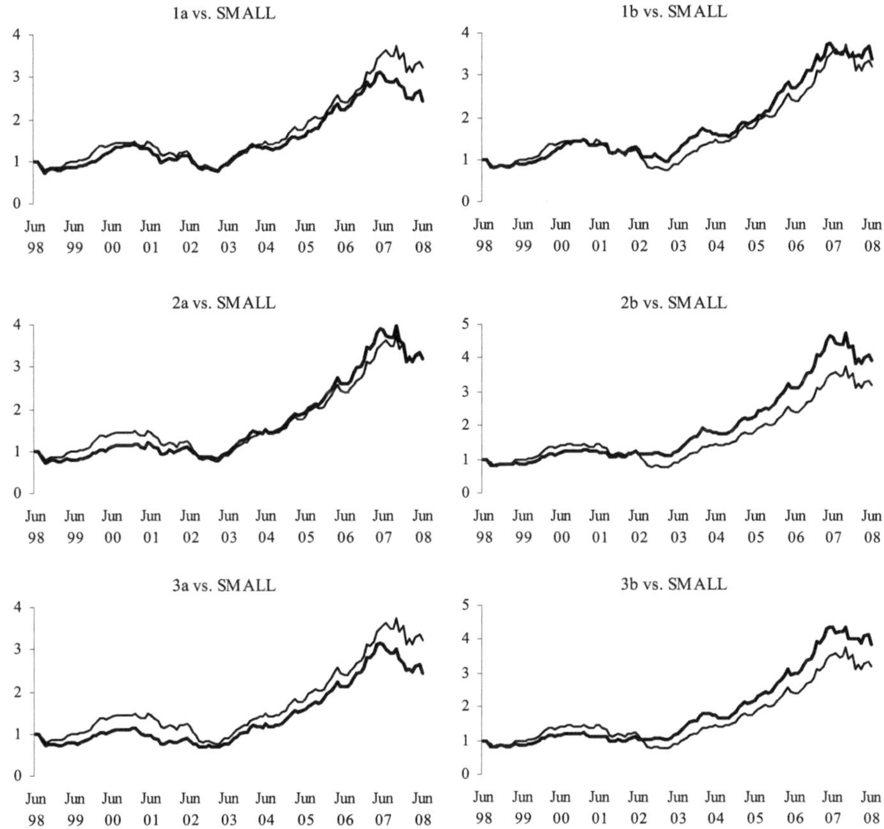

Figure 7: Cumulative returns of active investment strategies I

The bold lines represent the cumulative return of the respective investment strategy listed at the top of each chart. The thin lines represent the cumulative return of a buy and hold investment in SMALL. The calculations are based on gross returns.

A3. Style Rotation Strategies (4a to 6b) vs. SMALL

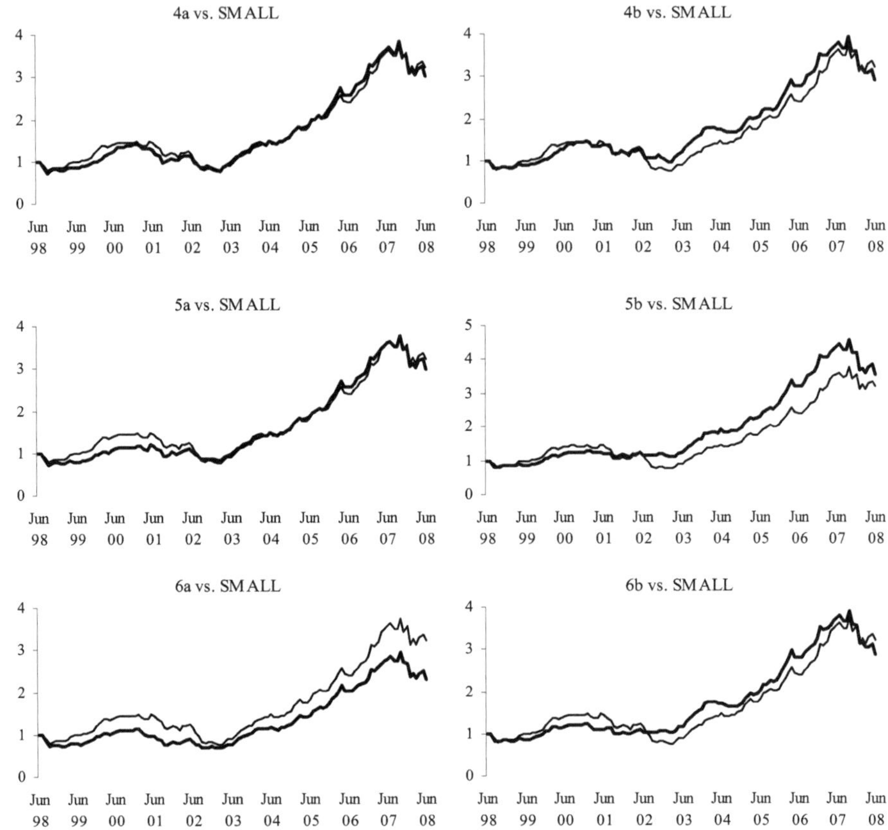

Figure 8: Cumulative returns of active investment strategies II
The bold lines represent the cumulative return of the respective investment strategy listed at the top of each chart. The thin lines represent the cumulative return of a buy and hold investment in SMALL. The calculations are based on gross returns.

A4. Style Rotation Strategies (1a_6 to 3b_6) vs. SH

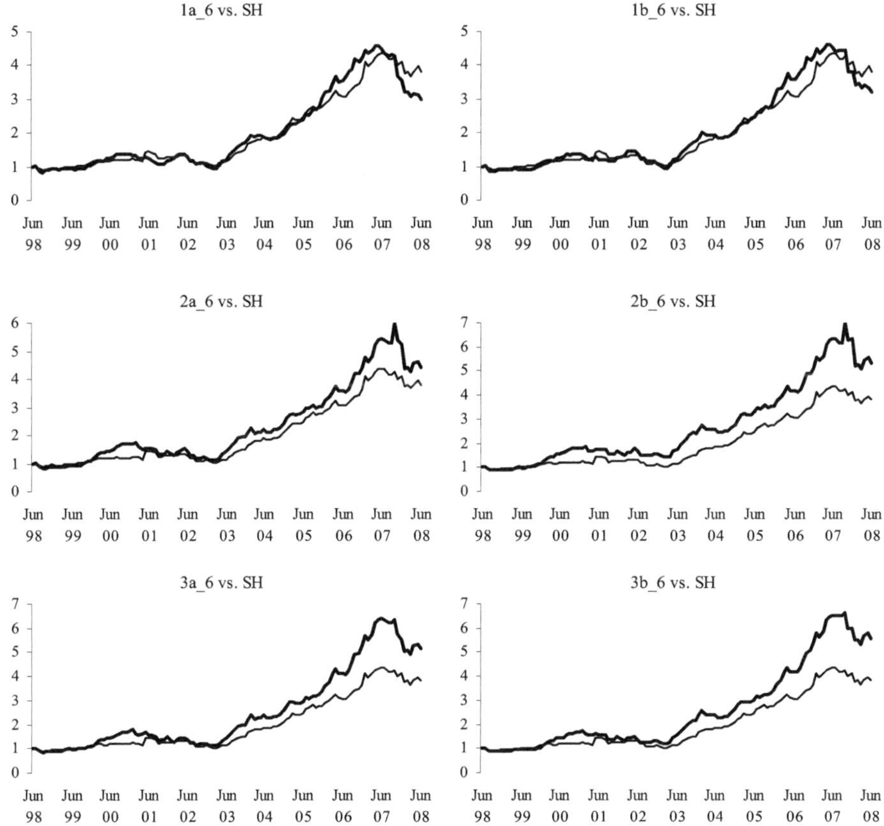

Figure 9: Cumulative returns of active investment strategies III
The bold lines represent the cumulative return of the respective investment strategy listed at the top of each chart. The thin lines represent the cumulative return of a buy and hold investment in SH. The calculations are based on gross returns.

A5. Style Rotation Strategies (4a_6 to 6b_6) vs. SH

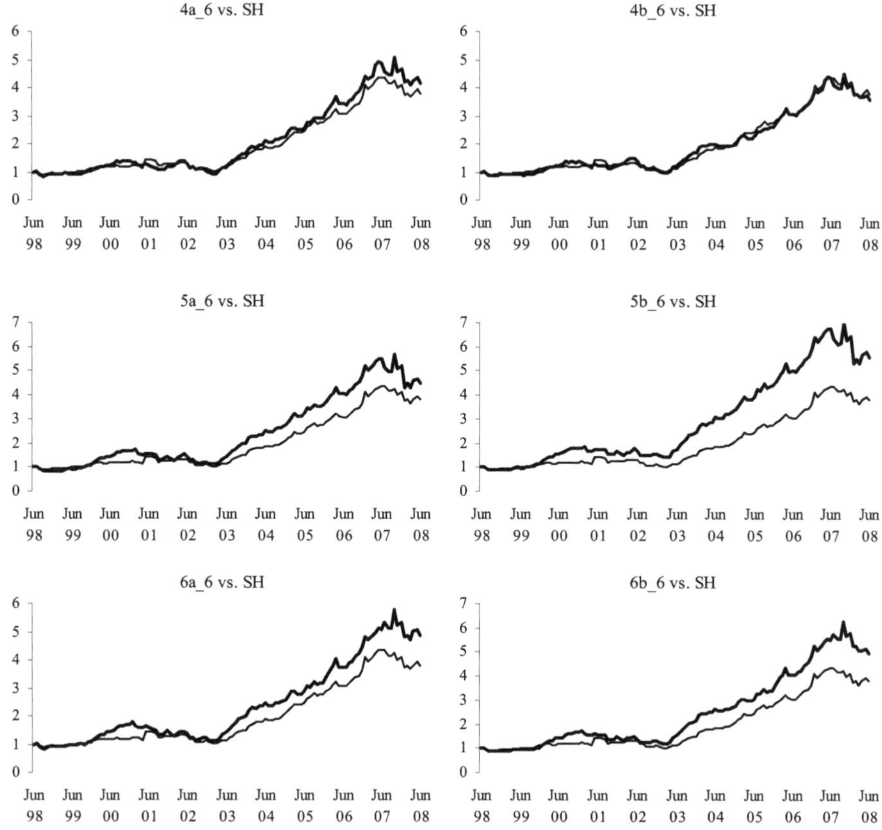

Figure 10: Cumulative returns of active investment strategies IV
The bold lines represent the cumulative return of the respective investment strategy listed at the top of each chart. The thin lines represent the cumulative return of a buy and hold investment in SH. The calculations are based on gross returns.

References

Ammann, Manuel, and Michael Steiner, 2008. Risk Factors for the Swiss Stock Market. Swiss Journal of Economics and Statistics 144 (1), 1-35.

Ariel, Robert A., 1987. A Monthly Effect in Stock Returns. Journal of Financial Economics 18, 161-174.

Arshanapalli, Bala G., Switzer, Lorne N., and Karim Panju, 2007. Equity-style timing: A multi-style rotation model for the Russel large-cap and small-cap growth and value style indexes. Journal of Asset Management 8 (1), 9-23.

Asness, Cliff S., Friedman, Jacques A., Krail, Robert J., and John M. Liew, 2000. Style Timing: Value versus Growth. Journal of Portfolio Management 26 (3), 50-60.

Bachelier, Louis, 1900. Théorie de la Speculation. Gauthier-Villars: Paris.

Badrinath, S.G., Kale, Jayant R., and Thomas H. Noe, 1995. Of Shepherds, Sheeps, and the Cross-Autocorrelations in Equity Returns. Review of Financial Studies 8 (2), 401-430.

Ball, Ray, and Philip Brown, 1968. An Empirical Evaluation of Accounting Income Numbers. Journal of Accounting Research 6 (2), 159-178.

Ball, Ray, and S.P. Kothari, 1989. Nonstationary expected returns: Implications for tests of market efficiency and serial correlation in returns. Journal of Financial Economics 25, 51-74.

Balvers, Ronald J., Cosimano, Thomas F., and Bill McDonald, 1990. Predicting Stock Returns in an Efficient Market. Journal of Finance 45 (4), 1109-1128.

Banz, Rolf W., 1981. The Relationship Between Return and Market Value of Common Stocks. Journal of Financial Economics 9, 3-18.

Barberis, Nicholas, and Andrei Shleifer, 2003. Style investing. Journal of Financial Economics 68, 161-199.

Bernard, Victor L., and Jacob K. Thomas, 1989. Post-Earnings-Announcement Drift: Delayed Price Response or Risk Premium?. Journal of Accounting Research 27, 1-36.

Bhojraj, Sanjeev, and Bhaskaran Swaminathan, 2006. Macromomentum: Returns Predictability in International Equity Indices. Journal of Business 79 (1), 429-451.

Bieri, Beatrice, and Klaus Spremann, 2009. Erklärt das Zyklusbeta Aktienrenditen? Kredit und Kapital, forthcoming.

Black, Fischer S., Jensen, Michael, and Myron Scholes, 1972. The Capital Asset Pricing Model: Some Empirical Tests. In: Jensen, Michael (eds): Studies in the Theory of Capital Markets.

Bodie, Zvi, 1976. Common Stocks as a Hedge Against Inflation. Journal of Finance 31 (2), 459-470.

Boudoukh, Jacob, Richardson, Matthew P., and Robert F. Whitelaw, 1994. A Tale of Three Schools: Insights on Auto-Correlations of Short-Horizon Stock Returns. Review of Financial Studies 7 (3), 539-573.

Box, G. E. P., and David A. Pierce, 1970. Distribution of Residual Autocorrelations in Autoregressive Integrated Moving Average Models. Journal of the American Statistical Association 65 (332), 1509-1526.

Brandt, Michael W., 1999. Estimating Portfolio and Consumption Choice: A Conditional Euler Equations Approach. Journal of Finance 54, 1609-1645.

Brennan, Michael J., Jegadeesh, Narasimhan, and Bhaskaran Swaminathan, 1993. Investment Analysis and the Adjustment of Stock Prices to Common Information. Review of Financial Studies 6 (4), 799-824.

Brennan, Michael J., Schwartz, Eduardo S., and Roland Lagnado, 1997. Strategic Asset Allocation. Journal of Economic Dynamics and Control 21, 1377-1403.

Brown, Stephen J., and William N. Goetzmann, 1997. Mutual fund styles. Journal of Financial Economics 43, 373-399.

Campbell, John Y., and Luis M. Vicera, 1999. Consumption and Portfolio Decisions when Expected Returns are Time Varying. Quarterly Journal of Economics 114, 433-495.

Campbell, John Y., and Robert J. Shiller, 1998. Valuation Ratios and the Long-Run Stock Market Outlook. Journal of Portfolio Management 24, 11-26.

Campbell, John Y., and Robert J. Shiller, 1988. Stock Prices, Earnings, and Expected Dividends. Journal of Finance 43 (3), 661-676.

Campbell, John Y., Lo, Andrew W., and A. Craig MacKinlay, 1997. The Econometrics of Financial Markets. Princeton University Press: Princeton, NJ.

Carhart, Mark M., 1997. On Persistence in Mutual Fund Performance. Journal of Finance 52 (2), 57-82.

Chan, K. C., 1988. On the Contrarian Investment Strategy. Journal of Business 61 (2), 147-163.

Chan, Kalok, 1993. Imperfect Information and Cross-Autocorrelation among Stock Prices. Journal of Finance 48 (4), 1211-1230.

Chan, Louis K. C., Chen, Hsiu-Lang, and Josef Lakonishok, 2002. On Mutual Fund Investment Styles. Review of Financial Studies 15 (5), 1407-1437.

Chan, Louis K. C., Jegadeesh, Narasimhan, and Josef Lakonishok, 1996. Momentum Strategies. Journal of Finance 51 (5), 1681-1713.

Chen, Nai-Fu, 1991. Financial Investment Opportunities and the Macroeconomy. Journal of Finance 46 (2), 529-554.

Chen, Nai-Fu, Roll, Richard, and Stephen A. Ross, 1986. Economic Forces and the Stock Market. Journal of Business 59 (3), 383-403.

Chordia, Tarun, and Bhaskaran Swaminathan, 2000. Trading Volume and Cross-Autocorrelation in Stock Returns. Journal of Finance 55 (2), 913-935.

Chordia, Tarun, and Lakshmanan Shivakumar, 2002. Momentum, Business Cycle, and Time-Varying Expected Returns. Journal of Finance 57 (2), 985-1019.

Cochrane, John H., 1999a. New Facts in Finance. Economic Perspectives, Federal Reserve Bank of Chicago 23 (3), 36-58.

Cochrane, John H., 1999b. Portfolio Advice for a Multifactor World. Economic Perspectives, Federal Reserve Bank of Chicago 23 (3), 59-78.

Cochrane, John H., 2005a. Asset Pricing. Revised Edition. Princeton University Press: Princeton, NJ.

Cochrane, John H., 2005b. Financial Markets and the Real Economy. now: Hanover, MA.

Cochrane, John H., 2006. The dog that did not bark: A defense of return predictability. NBER Working Paper.

Conrad, Jennifer, and Gautam Kaul, 1988. Time-Variation in Expected Returns. Journal of Business 61 (4), 409-425.

Conrad, Jennifer, and Gautam Kaul, 1998. An Anatomy of Trading Strategies. Review of Financial Studies 11 (3), 489-519.

Conrad, Jennifer, Gultekin, Mustafa N., and Gautam Kaul, 1997. Profitability of Short-Term Contrarian Strategies: Implications for Market Efficiency. Journal of Business and Economic Statistics 15 (3), 379-386.

Cross, Frank, 1973. The Behavior of Stock Prices on Fridays and Mondays. Financial Analysts Journal 29 (6), 67-69.

Daniel, Kent, Grinblatt, Mark, Titman, Sheridan, and Russ Wermers, 1997. Measuring Mutual Fund Performance with Characteristic-Based Benchmarks. Journal of Finance 52 (3), 1035-1058.

Davis, James L., 2001. Mutual Fund Performance and Manager Style. Financial Analysts Journal 57 (1), 19-27.

De Bondt, Werner F.M., and Richard Thaler, 1985. Does the Stock Market Overreact? Journal of Finance 40 (3), 793-805.

De Bondt, Werner F.M., and Richard Thaler, 1987. Further Evidence on Investor Overreaction and Stock Market Seasonality. Journal of Finance 42 (3), 557-581.

Fama, Eugene F., 1965. The Behavior of Stock-Market Prices. Journal of Business 38 (1), 34-105.

Fama, Eugene F., 1970. Efficient Capital Markets: A Review of Theory and Empirical Work. Journal of Finance 25, 383-417.

Fama, Eugene F., 1981. Stock Returns, Real Activity, Inflation, and Money. American Economic Review 71 (4), 545-565.

Fama, Eugene F., 1990. Stock Returns, Expected Returns, and Real Activity. Journal of Finance 45 (4), 1089-1108.

Fama, Eugene F., 1991. Efficient Capital Markets: II. Journal of Finance 46, 1575-1617.

Fama, Eugene F., and Kenneth R. French, 1988a. Permanent and Temporary Components of Stock Prices. Journal of Political Economy 96 (2), 246-273.

Fama, Eugene F., and Kenneth R. French, 1988b. Dividend Yields and Expected Stock Returns. Journal of Financial Economics 22, 3-25.

Fama, Eugene F., and Kenneth R. French, 1989. Business Conditions and Expected Returns on Stocks and Bonds. Journal of Financial Economics 25, 23-49.

Fama, Eugene F., and Kenneth R. French, 1992. The Cross-Section of Expected Stock Returns. Journal of Finance 47 (2), 427-465.

Fama, Eugene F., and Kenneth R. French, 1993. Common risk factors in the returns on stocks and bonds. Journal of Financial Economics 33, 3-56.

Fama, Eugene F., and Kenneth R. French, 1995. Size and Book-to-Market Factors in Earnings and Returns. Journal of Finance 50 (1), 131-155.

Fama, Eugene F., and Kenneth R. French, 1996. Multifactor Explanations of Asset Pricing Anomalies. Journal of Finance 51 (1), 55-84.

Fama, Eugene F., and Kenneth R. French, 1998. Value versus Growth: The International Evidence. Journal of Finance 53 (6), 1975-1999.

Fama, Eugene F., and Kenneth R. French, 2006. The Value Premium and the CAPM. Journal of Finance 61 (5), 2163-2185.

Fama, Eugene F., and Kenneth R. French, 2007a. Migration. Financial Analysts Journal 63 (3), 48-58.

Fama, Eugene F., and Kenneth R. French, 2007b. The Anatomy of Value and Growth Stock Returns. Financial Analysts Journal 63 (6), 44-54.

Fama, Eugene F., and James MacBeth, 1973. Risk, Return, and Equilibrium: Empirical Tests. Journal of Political Economy 81 (3), 607-636.

Fama, Eugene F., and G. William Schwert, 1977. Asset Returns and Inflation. Journal of Financial Economics 5, 115-146.

Ferson, Wayne E., and Campbell R. Harvey, 1991. The Variation of Economic Risk Premiums. Journal of Political Economy 99 (2), 385-415.

Fisher, Lawrence, 1966. Some new stock-market indexes. Journal of Business 39, 191-225.

Foster, George, Olsen, Chris, and Terry Shevlin, 1984. Earnings Releases, Anomalies, and the Behavior of Security Prices. Accounting Review 59 (4), 574-603.

French, Kenneth R., 1980. Stock Returns and the Weekend Effect. Journal of Financial Economics 8, 55-69.

Gerlow, Mary E., Irwin, Scott H., and Te-Ru Liu, 1993. Economic evaluation of commodity price forecasting models. International Journal of Forecasting 9, 387-397.

Gibbons, Michael R., and Patrick Hess, 1981. Day of the Week Effects and Asset Returns. Journal of Business 54 (4), 579-596.

Goyal, Amit, and Ivo Welch, 2003. Predicting the Equity Premium with Dividend Ratios. Management Science 49, 639-654.

Goyal, Amit, and Ivo Welch, 2006. A Comprehensive Look at The Empirical Performance of Equity Premium Prediction. Working Paper.

Grinold, Richard C., and Ronald N. Kahn, 1995. Active Portfolio Management. McGraw-Hill: New York, NY.

Grossman, Sanford J., and Joseph E. Stiglitz, 1980. On the Impossibility of Informationally Efficient Markets. American Economic Review 70 (3), 393-408.

Hameed, Allaudeen, 1997. Time-Varying Factors and Cross-Autocorrelations in Short-Horizon Stock Returns. Journal of Financial Research 20 (4), 435-458.

Heaton, John, and Deborah Lucas, 2000. Portfolio Choice and Asset Prices: The Importance of Entrepreneurial Risk. Journal of Finance 55 (3), 1163-1198.

Hong, Harrison, and Jeremy C. Stein, 1999. A Unified Theory of Underreaction, Momentum Trading, and Overreaction in Asset Markets. Journal of Finance 54 (6), 2143-2184.

Hvidkjaer, Soeren, 2006. A Trade-Based Analysis of Momentum. Review of Financial Studies 19 (2), 457-491.

Jaffe, Jeffrey, and Gershon Mandelker, 1976. The "Fisher-Effect" for Risky Assets: An Empirical Investigation. Journal of Finance 31 (2), 447-458.

Jaffe, Jeffrey, and Randolph Westerfield, 1985. The Week-End Effect in Common Stock Returns: The International Evidence. Journal of Finance 40 (2), 433-454.

Jegadeesh, Narasimhan, 1990. Evidence of Predictable Behavior of Security Returns. Journal of Finance 45 (3), 881-898.

Jegadeesh, Narasimhan, 1991. Seasonality in Stock Price Mean Reversion: Evidence from the US and the UK. Journal of Finance 46 (4), 1427-1444.

Jegadeesh, Narasimhan, and Sheridan Titman, 1993. Returns to Buying Winners and Selling Losers: Implications for Stock Market Efficiency. Journal of Finance 48 (1), 65-91.

Jegadeesh, Narasimhan, and Sheridan Titman, 2001. Profitability of Momentum Strategies: An Evaluation of Alternative Explanations. Journal of Finance 56 (2), 699-720.

Jegadeesh, Narasimhan, and Sheridan Titman, 2002. Cross-Sectional and Time-Series Determinants of Momentum Returns. Review of Financial Studies 15 (1), 143-157.

Jensen, Michael C., 1968. The Performance of Mutual Funds in the Period 1945-1964. Journal of Finance 23 (2), 389-416.

Jensen, Michael C., 1969. Risk, the Pricing of Capital Assets, and the Evaluation of Investment Portfolios. Journal of Business 42 (2), 167-185.

Jensen, Michael C., 1978. Some Anomalous Evidence Regarding Market Efficiency. Journal of Financial Economics 6, 95-101.

Keim, Donald B., 1983. Size-Related Anomalies and Stock Return Seasonality. Journal of Finance 12, 13-32.

Keim, Donald B., and Robert F. Stambaugh, 1984. A Further Investigation of the Weekend Effect in Stock Returns. Journal of Finance 39 (3), 819-834.

Kendall, Maurice G., 1953. The Analysis of Economic Time-Series, Part I: Prices. Journal of the Royal Statistical Society 96, 11-25.

Kent, Daniel, Hirshleifer, David, and Avanidhar Subrahmanyam, 1998. Investor Psychology and Security Market Under- and Overreactions. Journal of Finance 53 (6), 1839-1886.

Korajczyk, Robert A., and Ronnie Sadka, 2004. Are Momentum Profits Robust to Trading Costs? Journal of Finance 50 (3), 1039-1082.

Kothari, S. P., and Jerold B. Warner, 2001. Evaluating Mutual Fund Performance. Journal of Finance 56 (5), 1985-2010.

La Porta, Rafael, Lakonishok, Josef, Shleifer, Andrei, and Robert Vishny, 1997. Good News for Value Stocks: Further Evidence on Market Efficiency. Journal of Finance 52 (2), 859-874.

Lakonishok, Josef, Shleifer, Andrei, and Robert W. Vishny, 1994. Contrarian Investment, Extrapolation, and Risk. Journal of Finance 49 (5), 1541-1578.

Lamont, Owen, 1998. Earnings and Expected Returns. Journal of Finance 53, 1563-1587.

Lee, Charles M.C., and Bhaskaran Swaminathan, 2000. Price Momentum and Trading Volume. Journal of Finance 55 (5), 2017-2069.

Lehmann, Bruce N., and David M. Modest, 1987. Mutual Fund Performance Evaluation: Comparison of Benchmarks and Benchmark Comparison. Journal of Finance 42 (2), 233-265.

Leitch, Gordon, and J. Ernest Tanner, 1991. Economic Forecast Evaluation: Profit Versus the Conventional Error Measures. American Economic Review 81 (3), 580-590.

Lewellen, Jonathan, 2002. Momentum and Autocorrelation in Stock Returns. Review of Financial Studies 15 (2), 533-563.

Lewellen, Jonathan, 2004. Predicting returns with financial ratios. Journal of Financial Economics 74, 209-235.

Liew, Jimmy, and Maria Vassalou, 2000. Can book-to-market, size and momentum be risk factors that predict economic growth? Journal of Financial Economics 57, 221-245.

Lintner, John, 1965. The Valuation of Risk Assets and the Selection of Risky Investments in Stock Portfolios and Capital Budgets. Review of Economics and Statistics 47 (1), 13-37.

Ljung, G. M., and G. E. P. Box, 1978. On a Measure of Lack of Fit in Time Series Models. Biometrika 65 (2), 297-303.

Lo, Andrew W., and A. Craig MacKinlay, 1988. Stock Market Prices Do Not Follow Random Walks: Evidence from a Simple Specification Test. Review of Financial Studies 1 (1), 41-66.

Lo, Andrew W., and A. Craig MacKinlay, 1989. The Size and Power of the Variance Ratio Test in Finite Samples: A Monte Carlo Investigation. Journal of Econometrics 40, 203-238.

Lo, Andrew W., and A. Craig MacKinlay, 1990a. When Are Contrarian Profits Due to Stock Market Overreaction. Review of Financial Studies 3 (2), 175-205.

Lo, Andrew W., and A. Craig MacKinlay, 1990b. An Econometric Analysis of Nonsynchronous Trading. Journal of Econometrics 45, 181-211.

Malkiel, Burton G., 1999. A Random Walk Down Wall Street. Norton: New York / London.

Mandelbrot, Benoit, 1963. The Variation of Certain Speculative Prices. Journal of Business 36 (4), 394-419.

Mandelbrot, Benoit, 1966. Forecasts of Future Prices, Unbiased Markets, and "Martingale" Models. Journal of Business 39, 242-255.

McInish, Thomas H., and Robert A. Wood, 1991. Autocorrelation of daily index returns: Intraday-to-intraday versus close-to-close intervals. Journal of Banking and Finance 15, 193-206.

Mech, Timothy S., 1993. Portfolio return autocorrelation. Journal of Financial Economics 34, 307-344.

Moskowitz, Tobias, and Mark Grinblatt, 1999. Do Industries Explain Momentum? Journal of Finance 54 (4), 1249-1290.

Mullainathan, Sendhil, 2002. Thinking Through Categories. Working Paper.

Nelson, Charles R., 1976. Inflation and Rates of Return on Common Stocks. Journal of Finance 31 (2), 471-483.

Perez-Quiros, Gabriel, and Allan Timmermann, 2000. Firm Size and Cyclical Variations in Stock Returns. Journal of Finance 55 (3), 1229-1262.

Pontiff, Jeffrey, and Lawrence D. Schall, 1998. Book-to-market ratios as predictors of market returns. Journal of Financial Economics 49, 141-160.

Poterba, James M., and Lawrence H. Summers, 1986. The Persistence of Volatility and Stock Market Fluctuations. American Economic Review 76 (5), 1142-1151.

Poterba, James M., and Lawrence H. Summers, 1988. Mean Reversion in Stock Prices: Evidence and Implications. Journal of Financial Economics 22, 27-59.

Reinganum, Marc R., 1981. Misspecification of Capital Asset Pricing: Empirical Anomalies Based on Earnings' Yields and Market Values. Journal of Financial Economics 9, 19-46.

Reinganum, Marc R., 1983. The Anomalous Stock Market Behavior of Small Firms in January. Journal of Financial Economics 12, 89-104.

Reinganum, Marc R., 1992. A Revival of the Small-Firm Effect: Far from Being Dead. Journal of Portfolio Management 18 (3), 55-62.

Roberts, Harry V., 1959. Stock Market "Patterns" and Financial Analysis: Methodological Suggestions. Journal of Finance 14, 1-10.

Roll, Richard, 1978. Ambiguity when Performance is Measured by the Security Market Line. Journal of Finance 33 (4), 1051-1069.

Roll, Richard, 1983. Vas ist das? The turn-of-the-year effect and the return premia of small firms. Journal of Portfolio Management 9, 18-28.

Rouwenhorst, K. Geert, 1998. International Momentum Strategies. Journal of Finance 53 (1), 267-284.

Rozeff, Michael S., 1984. Dividend Yields Are Equity Risk Premiums. Journal of Portfolio Management 11 (1), 68-75.

Rozeff, Michael S., and William R. Kinney Jr., 1976. Capital Market Seasonality: The Case of Stock Market Returns. Journal of Financial Economics 3, 379-402.

Samuelson, Paul A., 1965. Proof That Properly Anticipated Prices Fluctuate Randomly. Industrial Management Review 6, 41-49.

Schnedler, Philip, 2003. Der Nutzen aktiver Portfoliostrategien. Dissertation, University of St.Gallen.

Sharpe, William F., 1964. Capital Asset Prices: A Theory of Market Equilibrium under Conditions of Risk. Journal of Finance 19(3), 425-442.

Sharpe, William F., 1966. Mutual Fund Performance. Journal of Business 39 (1), 119-138.

Sharpe, William F., 1992. Asset Allocation: Management Style and Performance Measurement. Journal of Portfolio Management 18 (2), 7-19.

Sharpe, William F., 1994. The Sharpe Ratio. Journal of Portfolio Management 21 (1), 49-58.

Shivakumar, Lakshmanan, 2006. Accruals, Cash Flows, and the Post-Earnings-Announcement Drift. Journal of Business Finance and Accounting 33 (1&2), 1-25.

Spremann, Klaus, 2006. Portfoliomanagement. 3. Edition. Oldenbourg: Munich.

Spremann, Klaus, 2007. Finance. 3. Edition. Oldenbourg: Munich.

Spremann, Klaus, and Patrick Scheurle, 2009. Kapitalkosten bei zyklischen Risiken. In: Seicht, Gerhard (eds): Jahrbuch für Controlling und Rechnungswesen 2009. LexisNexis: Wien, 361-382.

Stattman, Dennis, 1980. Book values and stock returns. The Chicago MBA: A Journal of Selected Papers 4, 25-45.

Swinkels, Laurens, and Liam Tjong-A-Tjoe, 2007. Can mutual fund managers time investment styles? Journal of Asset Management 8 (2), 123-132.

Tinic, Seha M., and Richard R. West, 1984. Risk and Return: January and the Rest of the Year. Journal of Financial Economics 13, 561-574.

Treynor, Jack L., 1965. How to Rate Management of Investment Funds. Harvard Business Review 43 (1), 63-75.

Treynor, Jack L., and Fisher Black, 1973. How to Use Security Analysis to Improve Portfolio Selection. Journal of Business 46 (1), 66-86.

Vaihekoski, Mika, 2004. Portfolio Construction for Tests of Asset Pricing Models. Financial Markets, Institutions and Instruments 13 (1), 1-39.

Vassalou, Maria, and Kodjo Apedjinou, 2004. Corporate Innovation, Price Momentum, and Equity Returns. Working Paper.

MIX
Papier aus verantwortungsvollen Quellen
Paper from responsible sources
FSC® C105338

If you have any concerns about our products,
you can contact us on
ProductSafety@springernature.com

In case Publisher is established outside the EU,
the EU authorized representative is:
Springer Nature Customer Service Center GmbH
Europaplatz 3, 69115 Heidelberg, Germany

Printed by Libri Plureos GmbH
in Hamburg, Germany